Performance

JULIAN HILTON
Lecturer in Drama,
University of East Anglia

MACMILLAN

KT-420-939

First published 1987 by
THE MACMILLAN PRESS LTD
Houndmills, Basingstoke, Hampshire RG21 2XS
and London
Companies and representatives
throughout the world

ISBN 0–333–38572–1 hardcover
ISBN 0–333–38573–X paperback

A catalogue record for this book is available
from the British Library.

12   11   10   9   8   7   6   5
03   02   01   00   99   98   97

Printed in Hong Kong

Contents

General Editor's Preface

In the past ten years, Theatre Studies has experienced remarkable international growth, students seeing in its marriage of the practical and the intellectual a creative and rewarding discipline. Some countries are now opening school and degree programmes in Theatre Studies for the first time; others are having to accommodate to the fact that a popular subject attracting large numbers of highly motivated students has to be given greater attention than hitherto. The professional theatre itself is changing, as graduates of degree and diploma programmes make their way through the 'fringe' into established theatre companies, film and television.

Two changes in attitudes have occurred as a result: first, that the relationship between teachers and practitioners has significantly improved, not least because many more people now have experience of both; secondly, that the widespread academic suspicion about theatre as a subject for study has at least been squarely faced, if not fully discredited. Yet there is still much to be done to translate the practical and educational achievements of the past decade into coherent theory, and this series is intended as a contribution to that task. Its contributors are chosen for their combination of professional and didactic skills, and are drawn from a wide range of countries, languages and styles in order to give some impression of the subject in its international perspective.

This series offers no single programme or ideology; yet all its authors have in common the sense of being in a period of transition and debate out of which the theory and practice of theatre cannot but emerge in a new form.

University of East Anglia   JULIAN HILTON

Acknowledgements

My debts in writing this book are considerable. The University of East Anglia granted me study leave to write part of it, and the ideas it contains I can scarcely call my own in any proprietorial sense since they have developed over nine years of teaching with friends and students. As always, the help of the Shakespeare Bibliothek at the University of Munich, and Dr Ingeborg Boltz in particular, have greatly assisted my research. Nicholas Brooke, Heinz Fischer, Elinor Shaffer, Tony Frost, Tony Gash and Ralph Yarrow all shaped my thinking, as have generations of students too many to thank individually. I hope they will regard this as a product of an ensemble I have been proud to belong to. To Malcolm Bolton I owe a great debt in introducing me to the art of word-processing, which has changed my life. Sarah Mahaffy has helped at every stage.

In the course of writing this book two valued friends died, Dr Anton Büchner and Frau Marie Schwertler. Anton Büchner gave me the inestimable benefit of his personal experience of over nine decades of theatre-going, reminding me that fashions in theatre criticism change as fast as fashions in the theatre itself. Marie Schwertler spent fifty years in circus and variety performing throughout Europe and North Africa as Little Peppi. She endured social ostracisation, political persecution and chronic ill health in her long career, yet never lost faith in performance. I admire and miss them both.

J. H.

Preface:
Shakespeare, Sonnet 15

When I consider everything that grows
Holds in perfection but a little moment,
That this huge stage presenteth naught but shows
Whereon the stars in secret influence comment;
When I perceive that men as plants increase,
Cheered and checked even by the selfsame sky,
Vaunt in their youthful sap, at height decrease,
And wear their brave state out of memory;
Then the conceit of this inconstant stay
Sets you most rich in youth before my sight,
Where wasteful Time debateth with Decay,
To change your day of youth to sullied night;
   And, all in war with Time for love of you,
   As he takes from you, I engraft you new.

Chapter 1

All in War with Time: To Perform or not to Perform?

Artists commonly console themselves with the thought that, while they are mortal, their art will endure. Horace claimed that his poems were more durable than bronze,[1] Shakespeare consoled his lover with the prospect of being engrafted new despite the wastefulness of time.[2] Performance, at once the most intense and least durable of all forms of artistic expression, fits uneasily into this model of art as an everlasting monument to its begetters. It is a collective, not an individual, art and, even now, when it is possible to immortalise performances on film or video, the essence of the art remains its liveness, its spontaneity and its ephemerality.

This book is a study of theatrical performance, concentrating on the generic nature of performance, not individual performances. It analyses the nature of performance time, space and action: it offers a model for describing and anatomising a performance; it examines performance as a mode of communication and it offers ways of understanding its overall cultural purpose. Underlying the whole work is an exploration of the central theatrical paradox: that a mode of expression so transparently manufactured and artificial is simultaneously the agent of the most intense perception we may ever have of the real. We can witness the exact process by which a performer – I use the term to describe theatre actors, dancers, singers, and so on – creates a role, dons its costume, puts on its make-up and enters the false world of the stage. We can know that all his gestures are rehearsed and his tones of grief and joy assumed: yet still when we witness him enacting them in performance we believe that what we see and hear is real.

A dangerous art

Therein, according to many philosophers and theologians, lies the danger of the performance art. Plato worried about poetry in general, and performed poetry in particular, because he saw art not merely as an imitation of the real, but in that the real itself was an imitation of the ideal, an imitation of an imitation. It was doubly suspect. It could corrupt youth with the falsity of its emotions, which were manufactured, enacted and unseemly. Grief, love, hate and desire were to be avoided by the good stoic in real life, let alone flaunted on the public stage. So Plato suggested banning poets from the ideal Republic, unless they could reason their way back in.[3]

St Augustine, an actor and playwright in his youth, in later life found these Platonic strictures highly attractive. In the name of Christianity, he went even further, seeing in theatrical display the manifestation of the devil and the worship of false gods.[4] In Augustine and Plato theatre found two powerful and deeply influential opponents and the moral and religious opprobrium which they heaped on it still has its influence today. Only since 1968, for example, has there been no theatre censorship in Britain, and the threat of the censor's blue pencil is morally, if not legally, still present.

The culture out of which Plato was writing did not share his hard-line attitudes, and for a century at least, during which the great bulk of what has survived of Greek tragedy was written, theatre was held in the highest esteem by the Athenian democracy. But for the most part performers have lived in ambiguous social regard, on the one hand admired, even adored, for their looks and talents, on the other hand seen as frivolous, dissolute and corrupting.

A didactic art

Behind the religious and moral debate with which Plato and St Augustine are associated lies the problem of the effect theatre has on its audience, a fear grounded in the recognition that theatre cannot help but have an effect. Plato's fear was that theatre would teach the young to accept bad moral habits. If they saw gods on stage patently enjoying making adulterous love to young nymphs and, worse, getting away with it, young guardians of the future Republic would be tempted to imitate them. Augustine, citing Plato, made the same point. Theatre's self-defence was based on the claim that by performing scandals one exposed them as such, purging the audience of any desire they might have to behave in like manner. By showing evil you not only draw its teeth but also educate the faithful in means of avoiding temptation and sin.[5]

Both philosophers, such as Aristotle,[6] and churchmen, such as the Jesuits,[7] have defended theatre on these grounds, developing theories of dramatic art as essentially purgative and restorative, purveying high truths and firm morals. Aristotle defends tragedy against Plato's attack by claiming for it a 'cathartic' effect, a cleansing of, or perhaps by, the emotions of pity and fear.[8] The medieval church fostered mystery and morality plays as a way of integrating the message of the gospel into what were still in essence pagan theatrical pleasures. The school play occupied a central place in the Renaissance curriculum. And the Jesuits adopted the martyr drama as a central, and highly effective, mode of theological propaganda.

Theatre is indeed a powerful didactic tool. But, as the contours of the debate between theatre as agent for good and theatre as agent for harm show, exactly what theatre teaches is open to completely contradictory interpretation. The queston is unanswerable. It is no different in essence from the debate that constantly continues about violence on television – whether its portrayal encourages people to be violent or whether it puts them off. The signs are that it can have either effect, depending on the audience.

A studiable art?

If, as I have suggested, performance is a live, spontaneous and ephemeral art, can and should it be studied? Performance can be studied in a variety of ways, ranging from visits to the theatre as part of a study programme to the integration of rehearsal and workshop techniques in the teaching-situation. Film and video have also made it possible not merely to record performances, but also to analyse them in greater depth and detail than is possible even in the live-rehearsal situation. There is a self-evident qualitative difference between the event itself and a recording of it, but, as recording techniques improve, the gap between the live and the recorded performance is narrowing.

The study of performance engages with two central cultural issues. First, it explores the way in which the imagined, or even ineffable, becomes the real; secondly, it explores the relationship between the real and representations of the real. The act of making an idea or fictional character come alive is an act of *incarnation*, of turning concept, or print, into sounds, and movements. One reason why the Christian church in particular has always found theatre a troublesome cultural manifestation is that its own theology, as expressed in the first verses of St John's Gospel, makes a similar claim for Jesus, as 'the word made flesh'. Secondly, performing a text is an act of *transmutation*, changing one system of conveying information, print, into another, performance. As such, performance is the point of connection between language and action. If any aspects of our culture should be studied, these should.

If performance can and should be studied, how is the study to be conducted? Attempts to arrive at even a set of descriptive aesthetic rules for recording performance have all so far lost their force in the complexity of the detail into which they have led.[9] Attempts to create scientific criteria for defining performance by seeking correlatives between the aesthetic and the neuro-physiological responses of performers and audiences generate so much data that no conclusions can be drawn from them, at least as yet.[10]

So, rather than approaching the study of performance through empirical observation of vast numbers of different responses to a wide variety of individual performances, we have, if only for reasons of tractability, to construct some working hypotheses about the more general cultural effect of performance, into which scientifically measured individual responses may at some later stage fit. These generalised hypotheses about performance as a whole will be underpinned by empirical study of what playwrights and other theatre-practitioners have sought to achieve through specific performances and texts, thereby, admittedly, giving their artistic intentions more weight than their audiences' reactions.

Aristotle's case for studying poetry rests on two premises. The first is that poetry is the highest achievement of the human spirit, and hence deserves to be studied if anything is to be studied at all. The second is that poetry embodies and illuminates general principles about humanity that historical detail necessarily obscures. In this sense, poetry is a good deal less complex than history.[11] For both reasons, Aristotle subsumes the study of history within poetry. Analogous premises may be offered for performance. Few human activities integrate more, and more varied, skills than performance, which demands physical, intellectual, aesthetic, technological, managerial and business abilities. The first premise, therefore, is that the analysis of performance may be justified as a study of one of the most elaborate behavioural systems man has invented. The second premise is that performance is not merely a historical, descriptive art, reconstructing history as poetry. It is also a conceptual art, imagining and constructing alternative but possible worlds. The third premise is that performance is not merely an *art of execution*, the re-presentation of the creativity of another, but an *art of origination* in which re-presentation is a means to an original end, the performance itself.

Perhaps the most successful resistance to studying performance comes from within the theatre itself, where study and entertainment are held by some to be incompatible objectives. The case is weak in two respects. First, the oldest teaching-maxim of all enjoins teachers to instruct by pleasing. This is what theatre does. But, secondly, the process of making theatre leads through rehearsal, itself a studying- and learning-process, which even the entertainers go through.

There is no contradiction between pleasure and skilled analysis. It is a pleasure to be able to understand how theatre works, and enhanced understanding brings with it enhanced pleasure. But even the case for theatre as escape begs the question 'From what?' Presumably we are escaping from what we think is the real world into something we might describe as fantasy or fiction – in other words, its opposite. In the Elizabethan mind these two states were described as *workaday* and *holiday*:[12] theatre enabled one to put off the clothes and mentality of the everyday and humdrum and enter a strange and unfamiliar state, often akin to a dream. This is far from the moral cathartic case of Aristotle, at least on the surface, but in fact a sense of cleansing, and of release of aggressions and frustrations through what Mikhail Bahktin has called *carnival*,[13] is common to both views of performance. In the very theory of 'escape' lies a complex and fundamental perception of theatre's social purpose.

So in studying performance we are learning how to be better entertained – by it and by doing it, bearing in mind that entertainment need not exclude hard work, discipline or close study. Learning to be a performer, an entertainer, involves all these elements. Performers will always be able to evade or rebut the censure of their critics if they exercise their craft as story-tellers, jugglers, tumblers, fencers, musicians, healers and magicians well.

The art of the audio-visual

But the art of performing well is not simply one of telling good stories. Books can tell good stories. Performing incorporates two other types of skill, which after a period of four centuries of relative neglect are once more in demand. First, the advent of film and television has shifted the base of our culture from a textual to an audio-visual one: the way we store and transmit information, the way we learn and the whole way we live are increasingly determined by audio-visual rather than textual principles. This puts the skills of reading and writing in the new, but old, context of their progenitive skills of watching and listening, as the theatrical text is part, but by no means the definitive one, of performance.

Secondly, for the reasons given by Shakespeare in the sonnet that prefaces this book, performance is our front-line weapon in the war with time. It would oversimplify grossly to suggest that all performance is a meditation on the passage of time and the transience of being, but Shakespeare for one was in no doubt that the constant re-enactment of his work was his most likely source of immortality. In this respect, performing arts are paradoxically less time-bound than plastic arts. The very fact that a given mode of performing *Julius Caesar* cannot precisely be repeated liberates contemporary performers of the work from any pressure to be archaeologically accurate. When we go to see *Julius Caesar* we go not out of historical piety and reverence for the memory of its author, but because we believe that Shakespeare's play still has relevance to us. When we stop believing that, we shall stop going. In this way Shakespeare's play lives continuously in the present, and renews itself with every new performance. This power of constant renewal is referred to at the end of Sonnet 15. It stems from the recognition that the role in theatre outlives the performer. Performances pass, performance does not. Performers die, the role lives. Julius Caesar may be dead, but every night, somewhere in the world, he is resurrected.

The elements of 'The Poetics'

In what is still the most widely influential work on dramatic poetry, *The Poetics*, Aristotle uses a mixture of empirical observation and logical inference to establish what the elements of dramatic poetry are and how they combine. I use a similar method to examine the headings under which a poetics of performance can be created. Aristotle's primary concern was with the composition of literary drama; mine is with the audio-visual composition of theatrical performance.

The six components of the dramatic poem that Aristotle identifies are plot, character, message or thought, diction, melody and, last of all, spectacle.[14] *Plot* is predominant because an action is a precondition of drama; and by 'plot' Aristotle means not just the facts of a given action, but also how those facts are presented. Corneille was later to describe this aspect of plot as the 'liaison of scenes'.[15] *Character* is placed second to plot, because, so Aristotle contends, only through or in response to action is character revealed. The *message* or *moral* of a play is what we in the audience, perhaps under guidance from the chorus, feel is the resolution of the confrontation of a given character with a given destiny. Both *diction* and *melody* refer to the aural texture of the poem, as well as to its grammar and syntax, so there is necessarily a performance element in these two, if not of a necessarily theatrical kind. Last is *spectacle*, which Aristotle thinks of as an optional extra.

When all five, or perhaps six, elements combine, they constitute what Aristotle defines as 'the imitation of an action'. Tragedy is a reconstruction through poetry, a re-presentation in dramatic form, of a past significant event, such as the rise and fall of Oedipus. Performance in these terms is seen as secondary to both the imaginative, poetic, act of reconstruction and also to the processes of reception a given audience goes through to obtain access to that reconstruction.

This Aristotelian perception of tragedy as an imitation of a past event may well be the reason why he seems to pay so little regard to performance *per se*, because nothing seems more ephemeral, more a victim of historical processes, than a given performance. In a literal way, it is hard to see how universal poetic truth and the brief hour of the stage can be combined. If tragedy is an essentially nostalgic art, predicated on regret and guilt at the loss of values once enshrined in an irretrievably lost golden age, then performance, which is so unashamedly present, can have no part in it. But it is most crucially here that the power of performance creates the link between past and present, by transforming the unit of historical time past into performance time present. Performance offers the simultaneous possibilities of experiencing *Oedipus* for the first time, of experiencing it as a historical event, and of experiencing it as a poetic re-enactment of a myth of central significance to our culture. Experiences such as these can exist in parallel: there is no perceptual or psychological law which forbids us the awareness of existing in two or even more temporal systems at the same time. Performance mediates between poetry and history, offering designated moments within time to explore the timeless.

Performance and the generation of myths

When the two forces, of the enactment of stories and of the ability to defy time, are combined, the product is myth: the story that is at once fictional, in the sense of being outside a documentary understanding of history, and real, in the sense that cultures define themselves by their interpretation of the meanings such myths generate. Hence Oedipus, Hamlet and Dr Faustus, none of whom existed in any literal way, are three of the most powerful individuals in our culture. Hamlet may not have lived at all, but in the minds of those who have witnessed his struggles he is far more real a presence than great aunt Doris whom we see once a year at Christmas, or any of his real historical contemporaries. More: myth in performance becomes incarnate; the performer becomes the tangible embodiment of a defining element in the collective consciousness. When audiences 'escape' to witness such acts of reincarnation, that process of escape deserves more attention than being written off as entertainment. Entertaining it must be. But this begs the question of why we find it entertaining.

Myths become eternal by being seasonal. Just as the season returns, so does the myth, often connected with a season, or festival day in the year. Seasonality is not merely a question of repetition: it also involves balance, the balance of winter and summer, spring and autumn. In the construction of performances and in their social functions, seasonal patterns will have a marked effect, because through seasonality performance explores one of the central temporal paradoxes of our culture.

This paradox is given expression in the connection Shakespeare establishes between the performer and time. The performer seems on the one hand to live in the continuous present and on the other to be part of a great seasonal cycle of birth and decay. In *As You Like It* he has Jaques elucidate the ambiguity of the word 'stage' in one of the most famous speeches he wrote. The world is a stage, but the world is always at a particular stage of development – always on the point of growing into something different from what it is now. This counterpoises two seemingly opposite forces in the seasonal cycle: individual death and generic life. The tension is resolved in individual melancholy – 'I must die' – and collective optimism: 'we shall grow'. The same is true for the relationship between myth-maker and the myth. The myth-maker is mortal, but his myth is infinitely retellable. Caesar is dead, but he is infinitely re-presentable.

Theatre, existing as it does in the continuous present, becomes the natural focus of living memory, to which every performer is a mouthpiece. It is a means of retaining in concrete form in the present the processes of cultural evolution which are in all other respects in the past. Through repetition and re-enactment of a given performance piece, a seasonal balance is struck between constancy and decay. The performer likewise enters a rehearsal process which is both historical and seasonal. His work is historical in that he creates a role within a finite rehearsal time. It is doubly evolutionary in that his creative effort contributes to an incremental growth both in himself and in the meaning of his role, a study in metamorphosis and mutation by which one consciousness – his own – enters a semi-permanent relationship with another: the role's. Unlike the Ovidian metamorphoses, where people are irreversibly transformed into flowers and trees, this metamorphosis is, in part, reversible. The actor playing Hamlet can return to his former self, though some traces of Hamlet may remain with him.

These processes do not happen by accident. They are part of an elaborate cultural system which is partly concrete and tangible in its nature, partly a metaphor of universal dimensions. To study this cultural system we need to consider what its components are, how they interact, and how they may be categorised and defined.

Chapter 2

This Huge Stage: A New Poetics?

Aristotle in *The Poetics* summarises his view of spectacle as follows:

> The spectacle has, indeed, an emotional attraction of its own, but of all the parts, it is the least artistic, and connected least with the art of poetry. For the power of tragedy, we may be sure, is felt even apart from representation and actors. Besides, the production of spectacular effects depends more on the art of the stage machinist than on that of the poet.[1]

One cannot claim that the tragic is exclusive to performance. But, in anatomising tragedy into text, acting and stage effect, Aristotle creates the impression of performance as a loose association of allied arts, rather than as a single integrative art in its own right. Gerard Manley Hopkins pointed out that poetry only is when it is read. My case is that plays only are when they are performed.

Aristotle's assertion has three flaws. The first, and most serious, is that it denies the independence of the performance art from the art of the dramatic poem. Sam Johnson, unrepentantly contemptuous of actors, ruefully admitted to Boswell that even poor scripts may produce fine performances, and so pinpointed the fact that there is no necessary relationship between the literary worth of a dramatic composition and its power in performance.[2] The second flaw is to conceive of the playwright's imagination as exclusively, or even dominantly, literary. The playwright's task is to integrate word and image, as the basis of a play. His script is just one part of an elaborate combination of aesthetic devices which together generate an audio-visual artefact. Aware of the complementarity of word and image, many writers give extensive stage directions as to how their works should look and sound; Shakespeare's plays have few explicit, but a wealth of implicit, directions – such as the comments characters make about the way each other look and sound.

The belief that performance is in origin a literary, textual art is nevertheless dogged, and one many contemporary critics seem to share in their use of the term 'performance text'[3] to describe the difference between performance of a play and the reading of it. In the view of performance that I shall be presenting, the text is to be conceived as (a) optional in the performance process, and (b) more a written record of what has occurred than a master plan for reconstructing an audio-visual event.

The third flaw is a subtler but damaging one. Performance is a popular public art. It is accessible to those who can neither read nor write. Reading is a private art, conducted alone. There seems to be implicit in Aristotle's position a classic rejection of a mass art form relatively easy of access in favour of a private one whose rules are comprehensible only to a few.

World stage

Shakespeare's belief in the special nature of performance is implicit throughout his plays and made occasionally explicit in speeches on the relationship between the world and the stage. In Jaques's disquisition on the world as stage, he pinpoints the interpenetration of theatre and world:

> All the world's a stage,
> And all the men and women merely players.
> They have their exits and their entrances,
> And one man in his time plays many parts,
> His acts being seven ages.
> > (*As You Like It*, ii.vii.139–43)

I am not suggesting a naïve identification of Shakespeare with his creation, although here I do hear Shakespeare's own voice. Rather, the key words, 'stage', 'play', 'part' and 'act', brought into a single statement, are all richly ambiguous, semantically integrating the world of performance with the world of real experience in the metaphor of the world stage.

Stage. There are three main senses in which the concept of a stage applies to performance. It is the term to describe the surface on which the actor moves, it describes a unit of measurement of indeterminate length, and it suggests metamorphosis or development. The physical stage is thus a flexible measure of a particular point of development in a metamorphosing mind.

Act. Like 'stage', there are three main senses in which the term 'act' applies to theatre. Plays are divided structurally into acts and scenes, the act being a unit of performance time, of indeterminate length. 'Act' describes an event or deed that occurs within that time. And it describes the psychological and aesthetic process by which one person assumes the role of another. The theatrical act is therefore an event or deed, taking a certain time conducted within certain aesthetic and psychological rules of representation.

Play. Consistent with the first two terms, 'play' has three main functions. It describes the sum of the acts of a performance, first in an administrative and secondly in a phenomenological sense. Thirdly, it indicates semantically that one major source of the representational system referred to above is playing games.

Part. Not to be left out, 'part' carries three major levels of meaning. 'Part' defines performance in terms of linear units, divided by entries and exits, but also in terms of role distribution. A play is a sum of various temporal and personal parts. 'Part' is also significant within the general *synecdochic* strategy of theatre, for it is crucial to the sense of wholeness of an action to represent it by the most salient parts.

The preconditions of performance

The performance process has to be understood partly in physical, partly in metaphoric, terms. The physical requirements are threefold: there must be a performing *space*, the performance must take a certain *time* and there must be an *actant*. By 'actant' I mean any person or thing, human or not, who or which participates in the action. Commonly the actant will be the actor, or singer, but it may equally be a puppet, or a building (as in *son et lumière*), or a disembodied voice, as in radio theatre. Most commonly, performances use a wide range of actants, from set through to performers. The space and time may theoretically be of any size and duration and the number and nature of the actants have no theoretical limit. In practice, however, there are acoustic and optical reasons why a space should not be excessively large: audiences are unlikely to tolerate over-long performances and will find a vast list of individual actants confusing.

Performance space, time and actant are recognisable as such because of implicit or explicit acts of *designation*. By 'designation' is meant that someone or something names, or points to, performance space, time and actants, so distinguishing between them and their non-performance counterparts. The procedure works on a binary principle that everything in the world off-stage has its performance equivalent. This is similar to the 'workaday–holiday' concepts described above. In practice it means, for example, that an actor may walk across what are patently wooden planks, point to them, saying, 'Look at the grass. Isn't it green?', and we see green grass under his feet. The performer depends on the willingness of all those watching and listening to collude with him in thinking wooden boards to be grass. They in turn depend on the performer's willingness to convey his belief in what he is saying, within the designated boundaries of performance.

Through such acts of designation a deliberate tension, or *dialectic*, is created between our sense that the boards are grass and our sense that they are not. The synthesis of this dialectic of truth and nonsense is that we start to consider a third possibility, that the boards *could* be grass, and that to the performer they possibly are. If we are prepared to admit the possibility of grass, then we have accepted the designatory principle, and have no need to see 'real' grass as an objective correlative of the performer's claim. This is not only cheaper for the production budget but also allows, or requires, each of us to paint in the grass in the shade and form we feel is most appropriate. So we are invited to share in the performer's power of designation.

Acts of designation create sets of *binary pairs* between the performance world and the non-performance world, pairs on which we are dependent for constructing meanings from performances. Thus through designation of performance space we become aware that performance space has the physical properties of real space, but is also distinct in function from it: performance time exists in real time, but is not bound by it; actants are susceptible of the same physical laws in and out of performance space and time, but may also transcend them. Our awareness of the one use of the space reinforces by complementary opposite the awareness of the other.

Space

Any space may be transformed into a performance space by an act of designation. In his book *The Empty Space*,[4] Peter Brook talks of the act of planting a stake in the ground as one defining a performance space. Designating the circle creates a boundary between the performer's space and that of the audience. This is the basic binary division of space on which all performance rests.

Often the act of designation is implicit in the way the performance space is built. When we read 'theatre' or, rather more ambiguously, 'studio' or 'workshop' on the entrance to a building, the sign tells us that performances are likely to take place in them. (If we are in hospital we may have a special view of the sign 'theatre'.) The presence of a large number of seats or chairs, all facing the same empty space, reinforces our sense of theatre, as do heavy velvet curtains, stage lighting and ice-cream vendors. Yet these factors do not in themselves constitute a performance: it is only when we have learned a more sophisticated set of rules about the way these implements are put to special use in theatre that we fully appreciate the extent to which they designate performance space. Nor are these rules transparent: regular visitors to the Wells-next-the-Sea arts centre will know that the Granary Studio is a theatre, but outsiders need first to learn that this is not a place of floury delights.

Performance is a public art, and to perform in any space turns that space into a public place. The way both performers and audiences perceive performance spaces will be determined partly by their general cultural expectations about the design and function of space, partly by the specific rules a given production establishes. On the other hand, this means we are concerned with *location* and on the other, with *shape*.

Location

There are three main categories of location for performance space: *neutral*, *occasional* and *dedicated*. Neutral locations are open and empty, with no evident fixed features, or even patterns of use. They tend to be public parks, common land, or large open squares. When theatre is performed in such locations it takes its place alongside sport, walking the dog, funfairs and grazing sheep. An occasional location is one where there is an irregular but not infrequent custom of performance – typically a large public building like a church or royal residence. It may even have a basic similarity to the interior design and layout of a permanent theatre, such as in a lecture hall or church, where rows of seats, facing in the same direction, all look towards some central focus.

Dedicated locations are reserved for the exclusive, or nearly exclusive, pursuit of one purpose, and for performance this means a theatre, opera house or equivalent. The dedication of the space may well proceed from some formal and public act of permanent designation, such as the hanging-outside of a sign with 'Theatre' on it, or, in the case of the church, a service of consecration.

The more neutral the characteristics of a location, the more it carries with it the spatial equivalent to what John Keats identified as the special quality of Shakespeare's work as a whole, *negative capability*,[5] that potential for a space to become metaphorically representative of any other space. But this means there is a built-in conflict between the understandable desire on the part of performers to have formally recognised public space dedicated to their chosen use for it – i.e. a theatre – and the aesthetic ideal of a performance space being as unencumbered and neutral as possible. So how can one square the circle of negative capability and permanent spatial designation?

One approach is that suggested by Jean-Jacques Rousseau in his *Lettre à D'Alembert*, where he describes the following prototypic space:

> Plant a stake crowned with flowers in the middle of a square, gather the people together and you will have a festival. Better still, make the spectators themselves the objects of the spectacle; make them into the actors so that each sees and loves his own image in the others and thus all will be better united.[6]

The performance location Rousseau suggests is neutral or occasional – the square may well be a market square, its primary associations functional. The first act of designation is the planting of a stake, which centres the space around it in a circle of potentially infinite circumference. Dimensions are calculated to and from the stake, and power is a function of relative distance from it. The second, more commentatorial act of designation is crowning the stake with flowers. The traditional value of the stake in Christian iconography is as a place of punishment and martyrdom through death by burning. The flowers, suggesting perhaps harmless flames, perhaps funeral offerings according to emblematic custom, here neutralise the savage aspect to the spectacle and turn it into a celebration.

Having centred the celebration on a stake, and ensured that the most democratic of forms, the circle, is established around it, the stake then becomes redundant, for it is now the people themselves who become the celebration. In this transition from a space centred on the stake to a space centred on people is an emblem of the transfer of political power from an absolute centre to a decentred democracy. Rousseau saw control of space as one of the fundamentals of politics, the then-absolutist norm being heavily centred, the holiday opposite an infinite set of interlocking circles of individual independence.

Rousseau's ideal has two main drawbacks. From the spatial point of view, an audience sat in a circle will on average see the actors' faces and have a good acoustic position only half the time. So the historical tendency from earliest theatre spaces onwards has been to arrange the audience and the performers in such a way that they face each other as much as possible. The locationary drawback to performing in the market square is the weather, so performers have used large indoor spaces, notably churches, instead.

Performing in church does, however, pose a problem. The locationary message conveyed by any space only occasionally used for performance is determined by its primary purpose, which for a church is prayer and worship. When plays are performed in church, their effect can be reinforced if what they are about and the way they are presented accord with the belief system enshrined in the space. T. S. Eliot's *Murder in the Cathedral*, written for performance in Canterbury Cathedral, is hard to imagine performed outside church, since the whole work is constructed on the locationary principles of the church as performance space. If, by contrast, the play performed is antipathetic to the church, it may obtain some assistance from the location by being in tension with it, but more probably the result will be to neutralise the effect of the play. This is one reason why churches do not convert well into theatres, because the locationary message they give out is always 'church'.

The complementary problem the dedicated theatre space has to face is cost. How in the case of a roofed building is a costly structure maintained? The problem is as acute today as it ever has been, and nearly always the answer has been subsidy, whether by the *polis* or the crown or the local council. The price theatre has had to pay for its subsidy has frequently been a high one in terms of aesthetic control.

A significant exception was the florescence of the London theatre after 1570. For in 1570 the Burbage family built what is regarded as the first professional, dedicated theatre space, called simply The Theatre. The design of this and subsequent buildings in this phase of theatre history was dictated by the need to make them profitable, within the economic context of continuing aristocratic patronage. Such theatres reflected their dual financial base – box office and subsidy – in their shape, covering the wealthier section of the audience and leaving the pit open to the sky. More intimate performances were, however, still going on in occasional locations such as the dining-halls of the inns of court, or guildhalls, which offered the advantages of interior space to audiences and performers alike. So was set in motion a historical process of professionalisation of theatre within dedicated spaces which has continued more or less uninterrupted to the present.

In our own time, the most original development in locationary attitudes to performance has taken place within the community- and alternative-theatre movement,[7] which has once more taken theatre back into the neutral and occasional spaces, into the streets, village halls, prisons, hospitals, old people's homes, schools and parks. Often the productions staged have suffered from being ill-conceived for such locations, but, at less cost and with broader appeal, such theatre has challenged at root the building-centred subsidy policy of many states. Might it not be better, as in the sixteenth and seventeenth centuries, to promote a better balance between touring and building-based theatre?

Shape and spatial organisation: proxemics

Within the chosen location, the shape and internal organisation of a performance space is our next concern, which may be defined as a question of *proxemics*.[8] Proxemics is the study of the cultural, sociological and psychological implications of relative distances, shapes and domains within space. To understand the significance of the cruciform shape and location of the Gothic cathedral, for example, we need to add to our understanding of its centrality and enormous size in relation to all other buildings of its period the fact that the cross is the most sacred emblem of the religion responsible for erecting the building and that the ground on which it is built is holy and of the highest status. We must also know that the cathedral's purpose is to enable all the celebrants in the building to see not each other, but rather the cross hanging over the intersection of the nave with the transept, below with their priest leads worship.

There are three main types of spatial organisation. These are *informal*, *semi-fixed* and *fixed*. By 'informal' is meant a spatial system with no rules of use and no obvious conventions of spatial distribution. In practice, however, few spaces are wholly free from such conventions. Parks and open fields are carefully organised spaces and have built-in conventions – 'Do not walk on the grass', 'Please walk round the edge of the field' – which determine our relationship with that space. Most human space is either semi-fixed, in that it permits of some variation in use and some obedience to convention and necessity, or fixed, in that its rules are completely defined and inflexible. The tendency is for authority to express itself in terms of restrictions on space – 'Staff only', 'This door not to be used by residents', 'Private' – and the more the restrictions the greater the evidence of the system of control. An equal tendency is for theatres themselves to grow into hierarchical and institutionally fixed centres.

ARRANGING THE SEATS

The theatre, seen within the proxemic system, combines all three modes. In its basic internal organisation it is a complementary pairing of fixed audience and informal performance space, with four semi-fixed ways of arranging the seats.

The closest to the celebratory ring is the *in-the-round* form, with the audience in either a square or a circle, totally enclosing the performing-area. In this model, the audience alone determines the physical boundary of the space, and the performers are seen against a background of other members of the audience. From the performers' point of view there are a number of drawbacks to this arrangement: they have to turn their backs on at least half the audience at any one time, and they then become harder to hear. There are other problems. There can be no large vertical planes in the set, because they would obscure the *sight lines*, the audience's view; and it is very hard to manage sudden revelations and *coups de théâtre* in the round, because of the logistics of making entrances and exits. Only the use of the floor trap, never a wholly reliable device, or the flying harness, never very popular with performers, can vary the pattern of entry and exit in the horizontal plane. The location of sporting spectacle, however, indicates that the in-the-round mode is the best one for involving the audience in the confrontational aspects of action. For if the backdrop to the drama is in effect oneself – a 'mirror image' of other members of the audience of which one is oneself a part – the sense of inclusion in the event is unavoidable.

Many of the problems of working in the round are removed by the *thrust* stage form. If one may conceive of in-the-round as 'in-the-square', the thrust stage is formed by removing one of the sides of the audience square and performing to the other three. The fourth side functions as a backdrop giving access to what Elizabethan actors knew as a 'tiring [retiring/attiring] house'. Working on the thrust stage, one still has a strong feeling of being enclosed by the audience, especially when right at the front of the stage, so it retains most of the advantages of the ring. Shakespeare's Globe used this form, the thrust of the forestage carrying the actor deep into the heart of the audience. The spatial arrangement of the Greek theatre is similar: the audience sat round the *orchestra*, the large circular area in the centre of the theatre. The main difference from Shakespeare's stage, however, was that the leading protagonists did not use the 'thrust', keeping the dominant action on the *scene*.

By removing the audience from a further side of the celebratory square, we create the least used of stage forms, the *traverse*, in which the action takes place down a corridor between the audience. This is structurally analogous to the medieval processional form, which can be conceived of as an enormously long traverse stage. It is seldom used indoors, because it appears to retain most of the disadvantages of the in-the-round form and not have its principal advantage, that of enclosure. In practice, however, the traverse can be a very useful way of staging plays such as *All's Well that Ends Well*, because the processional ancestry of the shape is appropriate to the portrayal of a journey or a quest.

In the evolution of theatre buildings, it has been the *end-stage* (or *proscenium arch*) form which has had the upper hand over all the others, at least in the past 200 years. The end-stage form removes from our notional audience square all but one side, leaving the audience in one half of the performance space and the performers, behind a picture frame, in the other. Some semblance of the celebratory circle is kept in the arched or horseshoe-like structure of the auditorium. But the principal purpose of the spatial system is to locate performers exactly opposite their audience. The reasons for the triumph of the end stage and the proscenium arch are matters for a different study from this one, but they have to do with the low social regard in which the actor was for so long held, and the curiously double morality of their audiences, who evidently loved going to the theatre but thought actors hideously immoral.

Naturally there were also positive reasons for the success of the proscenium. It solved the major visual and acoustic problems of theatre architecture – within, that is, a view of theatre that treats it as an art of moving and speaking pictures. The audience is able to see and hear all that goes on, and end-staging offers the scenic designer what the in-the-round shape denies: use of the vertical plane, and in particular perspective. Now that cinema has taken the art of moving and speaking pictures well beyond the technical capacity of live theatre to imitate, the proscenium form is in marked decline, and the inclusive, celebratory form has reasserted itself in new theatre-building.

In recent years a number of experiments have been made to locate the audience in more interesting and diverse directions. In *1789*, performed by the Théâtre du Soleil, the audience is in the centre of the performance space, and the performance goes on on stages around them. In other words, the audience moves. In an attempt to make coherent sense of the staging and dramaturgical problems of *Woyzeck*, Foco Novo moved their audience around the rooms of a large house, each room set for a different scene in the play. In concept, these devices are not new: the staging of medieval cycles, which structurally resemble *Woyzeck*, used a variety of

'places', or 'houses', each one being a distinct location in the drama.
Rather than the set having to change, the audience's focus of
attention merely moved from the 'place' of heaven to that of earth,
or hell. In Bill Bryden's production of *The Mysteries*, the audience
was moved around by the performers, so becoming a fluid, human
setting.

Another fruitful source of spatial innovation is the club or
cabaret, where, for reasons of sheer size as well as aesthetic
preference, rigid audience–actor boundaries are hard to draw: the
performance space is the whole environment.

SPATIAL ZONES

While stage shape has a significant effect on audience–performer
relations, relationships between performers and audience within
space are of greater consequence during the performance itself.
Taking the individual as the centre of concentric zones of space,
Hall divides proxemic relations between people into four main
categories: *intimate*, *personal*, *social* and *public*.[9] The exact
dimensions of these zones is variable according to culture – which
can lead to misunderstandings. Germans, for example, tend to talk
more loudly than the English, with the result that the English tend,
quite wrongly, to think of them as brash and argumentative, a
conclusion drawn from the dynamic level of their speech rather than
its content.

The intimate zone covers from direct touch and skin contact to a
distance of approximately 18 inches from the body. Within this zone
it is hard to converse with more than one person, and the presence
of another person within one's intimate zone implies either
considerable trust or aggression. Personal relationships may be
gauged by who is permitted entry to whose intimate space, and the
right of one person to enter another's intimate space may not be
complementary. The lord may enter the serf's space, or box his
servant about the ears. The reverse is not true.

Intimate space itself may be divided into two areas: in front and
behind the body. In front, there is a feeling of control and security;
behind, of vulnerability and weakness. Friends 'protect each other's
backs'; villains 'stab us in the back' when they have won our
confidence.

The personal zone covers from about 18 inches to 4 feet. Within
this area trust is still a significant factor, but no longer as powerful as

within intimate space. Personal space may be that inhabited by two friends in conversation, or even a small group. As with intimate space, it has a strongly exclusive sense to it to anyone observing from outside, and admission of new people to shared personal space will tend to be either on the basis of pre-existing friendship or of some explicit process of admission, such as a formal introduction. Conversations at normal vocal level can be carried out.

Social space covers the wider range of from 4 to about 12 feet, a space in which a relatively large number can sit, especially if 12 feet is the diameter of a circle. Yet the area is still coherent enough to feel in some sense exclusive. It may be significant that many rooms in terraced houses are built to a scale of between 11 and 14 feet, just on the boundary between social and public space.

Public space begins at about 12 feet, ranging outwards to about 25 feet. In the large nineteenth-century opera house, the pit alone may be nearly this wide, which underlines the extent to which the audience were then removed from the stage. By contrast, one of the successful theatres in Britain in the past decade is the Royal Exchange, Manchester, which achieves the proxemically remarkable, and desirable, feat of seating 700 people at a maximum distance of 30 feet from the stage.

The boundaries of all these zones may be breached or redefined by special circumstance, or specific convention. Intimate space is by its very nature private and exclusive. Yet in the rush hour we may well be squashed together with many unknown people in a train or a bus. We may react to this with a feeling of claustrophobic dislike, but we do not feel a threat to our personal status merely by the unbidden entry of someone else into our intimate space. The expectation that one will be squashed in the rush hour overrides the intimate proxemic code. Parties may likewise quite deliberately be premissed on breaking down proxemic barriers, either by formal introductions, or by devices such as round dances and random pairing.

These overriding-mechanisms are psychologically very useful for performance, for two performers may well be required to be highly intimate without actually liking each other at all. By designating the intimate space intimate within the terms of the performance it is at least easier, if not actually easy, to override innate spatial habits. That said, intimate touch is the most complex and difficult work in any rehearsal, for this is the area of greatest social taboo.

When we consider proxemic relations in the theatre, we encounter yet another paradox. For during the performance the group which spends its whole time in intimate space, shoulder to shoulder, is the audience. The width of the average seating-position is 18 inches, and the gap between rows about twice that. The performers, by contrast, spend most of their time in the middle two zones, personal and social. The spatial zone common to both groups is the public one.

Protected by the social convention of sitting shoulder-to-shoulder in the theatre, members of an audience see nothing special in what they are doing, whereas when they see one actor entering another's intimate space they know immediately something important is about to occur. Yet it does matter that members of an audience are in a constantly intimate relationship with each other, determined by the seating-arrangement. By virtue of the network of intimate spaces that sitting closely together generates, the audience becomes socially bonded with a shared identity and purpose. From this physical community comes *communitas* – that is, a sense of belonging to and communion with a vast group consciousness. If, as a result of seats being unsold, or poor organisation of the seating, there are endless ruptures in the net, this process is necessarily severely impaired.

We know relatively little about the reasons for certain behavioural characteristics during productions, by audiences under the influence of a sense of *communitas*. It has been established, however, that they tend to breathe synchronously with the performers and experience emotional and hence metabolic changes as a result of what they watch. Successful rock concerts induce states of elation, or hysteria, and can leave an audience feeling high for hours or days afterwards. This is perhaps the cathartic feeling Aristotle sought. Drugs may also stimulate the breaking-down of behavioural and spatial barriers, and hence lead to greater freedom of expression. For example, the festival of Dionysus, out of which Attic theatre is thought to have emerged, is a wine festival, wine playing a significant literal and metaphorical part in cult rites as well as contributing directly to breaching taboos of intimacy and touch.

SENSORY ZONES

Spatial zones are complemented by the sensory zones of each individual, which function likewise in concentric circles. In increasing order of spatial magnitude these zones are taste, touch, smell, sound and sight. Performance concerns itself primarily with sight and sound on the part of the audience, and sight, sound and touch on the part of the performers. Attempts have been made to engage the audience's senses of touch, smell and taste in performance, especially in performance art and happenings, and one could argue that the Wagnerian ideal of the *total art work* (*Gesamtkunstwerk*) should logically embrace all five senses. Performers never seem to object when there is eating or drinking to be done on stage. From the performer's point of view, sensitivity to all five senses is a priority in training, but such sensitivity involves the examination and breaking-down of complex personal and social taboos. This makes the work both difficult and alienating.

REACHING THE AUDIENCE
Historically there have been two strategies for reaching audiences, going to them, and letting them come to you. Both tended to try to be an inclusive as possible. The great theatres of Athens and Epidauros were designed to accommodate as many of the *freemen* of the polis as possible, as many as 15,000 people. The distances across which performances had to be projected far exceeded the outer dimension of public space, but great skill in building and brilliance in acoustic control meant that large numbers could see and hear well. Masks and larger-than-life costumes and effects would have further helped compensate for the loss of clarity engendered over distance.

The alternative to bringing the whole community to the theatre was to carry the theatre around the community on carts, the medieval processional style of performance. This meant that, although the community could no longer experience itself as a single body, the performance itself was made more accessible to individuals. Further, the processional style in itself acted as an agent of community, the performers creating a bond between the various groups of their audience by processing between them.

In *Henry V*, Shakespeare makes a conceptual leap to combine the virtues of the classical and the medieval playing-style:

> Linger your patience on, and we'll digest
> Th'abuse of distance, force a play.
> The sum is paid, the traitors are agreed,

> The King is set from London, and the scene
> Is now transported, gentles, to Southampton;
> There is the play-house now, there must you sit,
> And thence to France shall we convey you safe
> And bring you back, charming the narrow seas
> To give you gentle pass; for, if we may,
> We'll not offend one stomach with our play.
> But till the King come forth, and not till then,
> Unto Southampton do we shift our scene.
>
> (II, Prologue, 31–42)

Now the whole Globe is in motion, without the audience having to leave their places: the scene may process without leaving its place. It has become a space–time machine, and as such the most powerful metaphor in our culture.

Time

Of all the conceptual problems theatre sets, the relationship between real time and stage time is the most complex. Talking of real time Shakespeare refers in *Henry V* to 'the two hours' traffic of the stage', a reference fraught with some difficulty as very few of his plays can be performed in under three hours without substantial cuts. Real-time conventions now have it that a visit to the theatre lasts about two to three hours, from about 7.30 to 10.00 p.m., leaving time for a visit to the pub or restaurant afterwards. It feels curious to go to the theatre in the morning, and theatre performances in the afternoon tend to be either for children or for pensioners and are given a special title, 'matinees'. Not that this practice of evening performance is of great age. Greek theatrical festivals seem from what we know to have begun at dawn and run on through the day till sunset, probably encompassing all the daylight hours. Performances in Shakespeare's Globe took place in the afternoon, and started at 2 p.m.

Performance time has two main features: imitation of real time, and the dramatisation of time, in which there is no constraint other than the willingness of the participants to believe in whatever temporal structure is said to be operating at a given time. This is the aesthetic equivalent of the principle of relativity, which conceives of time in terms of relative speed in space. Real-time conventions are used as dramatic devices to give a sense of urgency to a task, and hence to generate *suspense*. In *The Comedy of Errors* Aegeon is told,

> Therefore, merchant, I'll limit thee this day
> To seek thy help by beneficial hap.
> . . . if no, then thou art doom'd to die.
>
> (i.i.151–2, 155)

The use of suspense is at once the most simple and most compelling tool available to the dramatist for securing an audience's attention. Will the bomb be defused in time? Will the pardon come too late? Will the villainous scheme be subverted? As a rule of thumb, time conventions in comedy are beneficent, in tragedy maleficent. In comedies the knot is always untied in the nick of time; but in tragedies pardons, forgiveness, revelations are always seconds too late. Othello is made aware how he has been deceived only seconds after he has murdered Desdemona, while Aegeon is rescued on the point of being executed.

Real-time conventions are used not merely for suspense, but also to reinforce the fact that time is passing, and hence that historical processes are in motion. Shaw tells us the date in *Caesar and Cleopatra* with great accuracy: '*An October night on the Syrian border of Egypt towards the end of the XXXIII Dynasty in the year 706 by Roman computation, afterwards reckoned by Christian computation as 48 BC.*'[10] The rest of the play is conducted with close attention to the accuracy of historical timing.

Suspense of a 'What happens next?' kind may be described as *primary* suspense and is balanced by *secondary* suspense, the audience's interest lying not with what happens but with why. Secondary suspense depends heavily on temporal relativity. In *The Winter's Tale*, Shakespeare explores an extended time scale, covering rather more than sixteen years in three hours, and most of this in sixteen couplets – during the speech of Time that prefaces Act IV:

> I that please some try all, both joy and terror
> Of good and bad, that makes and unfolds error
> Now take upon me in the name of Time

> To use my wings. Impute it not a crime
> To me or my swift passage that I slide
> O'er sixteen years . . .

(IV.i.1–6)

There are two reasons why this is acceptable to an audience. First, they will accept that in the sixteen years so rapidly passed over nothing of significance occurs. Secondly, in performance, any unit of time may stand for any other, meaning that the events of significance Shakespeare chooses to show imply all those he does not. Taken together these open up a third temporal possibility: that even units of time themselves are elastic and may at will be contracted, as in the last scene of *Dr Faustus*, or expanded, as in *The Comedy of Errors*, when the clock actually goes back an hour:

> DROMIO OF SYRACUSE.   . . . 'tis time that I were gone.
> It was two ere I left him, and now the clock strikes one.
> ADRIANA.   The hours come back! That did I never hear.

(IV.ii.53–5)

Aegeon has a friendly clock on his side. Dr Faustus, by contrast, has not. His real-time compact with Mephistophilis, giving him twenty-four years of special powers, not only passes within the three hours' playing-time of the play, but, in the climactic scene, hours slide by menacingly in seconds.[11]

A more complex relativity is used by Büchner in *Leonce and Lena:*

> GOVERNESS.   The day must have a spell on it. The sun won't go down and it's such an eternally long time since we fled.
> LENA.   But no, my dear, the flowers that I picked in parting as we left the garden are hardly wilted. . . .
> GOVERNESS.   It's getting late.
> LENA.   Yes, the plants fold their lilac-leaves together in sleep and the sunbeams rock themselves on the grass-stalks like tired dragon flies. (II.i)[12]

The objective correlative of the flowers is first used to disprove the governess's temporal assertion that they have been on the run for ever, and then, by an almost instant reversal, it is the flowers that seem to disobey temporal conventions by being still fresh at the end of a very long and hot day.

Actant

As with space and time, the most obvious purpose of the process of designation is to distinguish between those who are performing and those who are not, which is most economically done by establishing a convention of who uses the performance space and who does not. This convention will be reinforced by special costume, make-up, and the assumed names and modes of address the performers use. So is generated the classic binary pairing of performer and audience. One of the more powerful aspects of designation is that any thing as well as any person can become an actant, a performer. The actant may be anthropomorphic, like the puppets Punch and Judy; but it may be an article of clothing, or a place. Further, by an act of designation the animate may become inanimate, and *vice versa*, an actor playing a chair for example, and a telephone becoming a character. Edward Bond's play *Saved* turns on the stoning of a baby. The actant is a piece of material, or perhaps a doll.

In his attempts to answer the question in practice of what the minimum preconditions for performance are, Samuel Beckett embarked on a process of aesthetic reduction which culminated in his play *Breath*. *Breath* demonstrates how performance can do without the physical human performer and still constitute a performance. In this work the curtain rises on a stage full of rubbish, to the sound of a child's cry – birth. Having taken about thirty seconds to rise, it then falls to the sound of a dying man's death gasp. All the essentials are present: space, time and actant – in this case the curtain, the sounds, the stage and the rubbish. The play as such will not be frequently revived, but it establishes a number of significant principles.

First, it underlines the significance of designation to our perception of what kind of event it is that we are witnessing. *Breath* is a play. It could, however, be described as a work of art and located within a gallery. The label 'play' decisively influences our perception of it as such.

Secondly, as so often with both Beckett and Shakespeare, the play's title and content are intended as comments on the interdependence of meaning in the real world and meaning on the stage. The raising and lowering of the curtain is like a slow inhalation followed by an exhalation, the proscenium arch gaping for a moment like a huge mouth. What we see in that mouth is a classic twentieth-century emblem, the world not as stage, but as garbage heap.

Thirdly, the play explores the relationship between words and things, which in the case of breath is particularly problematic, since the word and what it represents are so ambiguous: breath is the essential condition of life and the image of hollowness. In *Macbeth*, Macbeth talks about 'mouth honour, breath', and Beckett's choice of title is characteristically resonant of this awareness of squandering what should be most precious to us.

Fourthly, the cry and the death rattle establish a seasonality and relativity to the theatrical use of time. Life is like a breath, life is a breath: a life-span is relativised into a single respiratory cycle.

Relativisation

The binary pair of designation – the act of definition and establishment of boundaries – is *relativisation*, which calls into question every boundary created. One way in which this is achieved has already been mentioned in Beckett's choice of *Breath* as his title, the pun. The pun makes one word carry two, or more, meanings, meanings which are often contradictory. The mere fact that one and the same linguistic sign, with one and the same phonetic constitution, can bear two very different meanings warns the writer that any act of designation, even with an instrument as sophisticated as language, is a potentially hazardous undertaking. Equally, as the arch-punster Shakespeare knew, the most economical way of subverting any linguistic boundary is the pun.

The same principle applies to the performance space, for the redeployment of the same real space to describe a potentially infinite number of performance spaces is analogous in structure to the linguistic pun. Hence, in the example I gave earlier, the wooden planks are simultaneously grass. Having given a space a specific location, the performer can then draw again and again on his power of designation to relocate us. But relativisation is not merely a process of repeated acts of designation: the relativity is of a more complex kind. Just as in real space and real time the concepts of

both are relative, so too, though in a more accessible fashion, are
the concepts of theatrical space and time. This issue is examined by
Shakespeare in *Henry V*, when in a chorus he explains the relativity
of the wooden O:

> Can this cockpit hold
> The vasty fields of France? Or may we cram
> Within this wooden O the very casques
> That did affright the air at Agincourt?
> O, pardon! since a crooked figure may
> Attest in little place a million;
> And let us ciphers to this great accompt,
> On your imaginary forces work.
>
> (Prologue, 11–18)

The space designated for performance can, through the active
intervention of the audience's imagination, hold the whole of
northern France, the casques of Agincourt, or whatever else
Shakespeare chooses. The wooden O is extremely elastic, more like
a huge and variable girdle – the image he uses in the very next line.
But the relativity has another aspect, that of the aural pun on 'O',
for not only is the O the circle of the Globe theatre, it is also the 'O'
of surprise – what German describes as an 'ah-ha' experience –
when the imaginary link is forged between two apparently
impossibly disjoint propositions. In this case space actually
becomes time, through its role as historical cipher.

Once the boundaries of space, time and actant have been
determined, the performance can infinitely vary and exploit the
dialectic of designation and relativisation. In this sense, theatre is an
analogue to the natural scientific concept of relativity, an aesthetic
equivalent to Einsteinian physics. Nor should this equation surprise
us. Shakespeare and his fellows chose to call their theatre the
Globe, which was intended to represent both literally and
emblematically the whole world. It was the artistic complement to
the great voyages of discovery that were encompassing the globe, an
attempt to realise the new dimensions of the world through
metaphor. The effort was no less arduous, and no less significant,
than the voyages of Magellan, Columbus, Drake and Raleigh.

Synecdoche and negative capability

The synthesis of the dialectic of designation and relativisation is the rhetorical concept of *synecdoche* and the metaphorical construct of *negative capability*. A highly popular renaissance figure of speech, synecdoche means the representation of the whole by its most salient or characteristic part, as the elephant by the trunk, or the king by the crown. What is shown implies all that is not shown.

While synecdoche tends to be a means of dealing with the concrete and the measurable, negative capability enables performance to make a quantum leap beyond the confines of the real world, and beyond the realm of what Aristotle describes as the probable. This is the most powerful of all theatre's tools, for through negative capability any unit of theatrical time and space, any performing agent, can stand in part or whole for any other. Any unit of time, of whatever length, may represent any other unit of time, any one space any other space. A performer may have a donkey's head, be a wall, or a moonbeam.

Two complementary processes are at work here, *intensification* and *transformation*: the act of designation by its nature intensifies our awareness of what is designated. We do not notice that real grass is green, because we expect it to be. We do notice the greenness of the grass when a performer points at brown floorboards and tells us they are green grass. Some acts of designation transform one thing into another. When we look at Snout acting a wall, we see patently that he is not a wall, and yet we see equally clear that he is. This opens the question in our mind of the extent to which Snout is a wall, and, further, under what conditions people become walls. In Mayan culture temple walls were built out of the skulls of countless sacrificial victims. The on-stage challenge to our perceptual conventions can have the effect of making us suddenly able to perceive things that previously were obscured to us. Common to both processes is a principle of economy of effort. Synechdoche is a powerfully economical way of conveying a lot of information in a short time.

Being and representing

In discussing the preconditions for performance I have so far stressed the practical and metaphorical aspects. What must concern us now is performance consciousness. In performance, a collective consciousness is generated in which all who are part of the event, in whatever capacity, share.

This collective performance consciousness is the reason why Joe Bloggs, who we know perfectly well is not Julius Caesar, can come onto the stage and convince us that he is. How is this possible? The answer has several aspects. To begin with, we the audience will have been instructed by advertising that a performance of *Julius Caesar* is to take place, where this is to happen and when. We may also have been told in the same process that Joe Bloggs is to play Caesar. Even if we do not know the play, we have a reasonable expectation that a play called *Julius Caesar* will have such a character in it – though having seen *Waiting for Godot* we may be wary about jumping to such conclusions.

When we get to the theatre, various acts and signs of designation will trigger our consciousness to expect that what we are to witness is a performance, in which we will see Joe. So, in Act I scene ii, we do; but the Joe we see is now Caesar. We know perfectly well that he isn't, but that within the play he is. Our performance consciousness asks us to believe two contradictory things about Joe, that he is and is not Caesar. If Joe does not manage to convince us that he is Caesar, we shall find the whole business pointless. If he manages to convince us so thoroughly he is Caesar that we forget he is Joe, we shall spring out of our seats to warn him of the coming danger. So Joe must accomplish the sophisticated feat of both being Caesar and merely representing him at one and the same time.

Matters are complicated by the fact that Joe, who is patently speaking English, is representing someone who spoke Latin, and that Joe's English does not sound like our own. Further, even could Joe speak flawless Latin of Caesar's period, it is highly unlikely that what he would say would bear any detailed resemblance to what Caesar himself said. What enables us, despite all these errors of fact, to accept the performance as authentic is the fact that events portrayed could plausibly have happened in the way shown. It is the same point as I made about the grass and the wooden boards. As long as Joe can convince us that things might have looked and sounded as he portrays them, then he satisfies our demands for plausibility of emotional and historical truth.

The dialectical relationship between being and representing becomes problematic in a different way when the correlative of historical existence is lacking, and the character represented is purely mythical – Hamlet or Dr Faustus, for instance. Characters such as these exploit negative capability most: for, because the performer is representing someone who has no original, he has a god-like power of calling into life a being who exists only in the collective imagination. This is the culturally most subversive aspect of performance, its capacity to transform potential worlds into real ones, without any prior basis in fact.

Consciousness and purpose

In opening up the question of the performer's ability to call life into being, we are returning to the relationship between theatre and religion; for in conceiving of theatre as a metaphor of the world we appear to be saying that theatre is in competition with religion as a model of reality and meaning. While Christianity offers certain ineluctable and immutable truths to the believer – that God exists, and that he is love – theatre will merely admit that he may exist, and that he may be love. It will also construct a potentially infinite number of other universes in which, for example, he does not exist. Christianity rests on orthodoxy, theatre on heterodoxy. In Christian belief it does not matter where you sit: you always have the best seat – in the sense of direct contact with God. In the theatre it does matter where you sit, and you do not see the same show as the person next to you.

Yet the history of performance in our culture is inextricably linked with relgion. Each partly defines itself by describing itself either through, or as not, the other; each has developed forms of behaviour that comment – by denial or acceptance – on the other. It would be inconceivable to think of Marlowe developing Dr Faustus as a character without the ghost of Luther at his side. But, now that we are living in as secular an age as there has perhaps been in our history, there is no longer intense rivalry between religion and theatre. This may have the effect of dealing theatre far more serious a body blow than television has or can. It may, on the other hand, mean that theatre has to rediscover some of its mythopoeic power, some of its ability to advance and enrich the collective consciousness independent of any religious system of belief.

Dynamic iconography

Whereas in iconographic systems associated with closed ideologies, such as Christianity, elements of the iconography have invariable meaning, as the cross signifies suffering and atonement, or the consecrated bread the body of Christ, in theatre iconographic meanings are variable. In the course of *Othello*, for example, Desdemona's handkerchief is an icon first of the love Othello has for her, then of his mistrust and finally of her fragility. The crown in *Richard II* changes from being an icon of power to being an icon of weakness and then one of power again. In this process, the iconography becomes dynamic. This dynamism is fundamental to the relativity of theatre, iconographic value being an attribute of the position in the play and the action in which an icon is used.

My use of the term 'icon' in this way is problematic, for the term has a more precise meaning within the study of sign systems, or *semiotics*. Semiotics works from the premise that all cultures generate systems of meaning encoded in graphic and textual sign systems, which function as an economic means of storing, retrieving and transmitting information from *A* to *B*. Sign systems are studied in three categories: *icons*, *indices* and *symbols*. The *icon* has a relationship of verisimilitude with that which it represents, as a photograph is an iconic signifier of the face. In the theatre, every performer has an iconic relationship with his role, in that his face is intended to signify the face of the character he is playing. Props are likewise icons, in that they resemble what they signify. The *index* is closest in concept to synecdoche, the part that represents, or points to, the whole. The murderer's dagger, itself an icon, points to the nature of the man. All stage action is necessarily indexical, in that, except in the rarest of cases, the real elapsed time of an action far exceeds the stage time taken to represent it. The third category of sign is the *symbol*, in which there is no necessary relationship between the sign, for example a linguistic sign or word, and the signified. 'Pain' in English means hurt, in French it means bread. Play texts are recorded in the symbolic system of print.

In its audio-visual nature, theatre is a dialectic of iconic and symbolic sign-systems, both resembling and representing the original action it signifies. The resolution of this dialectic lies in its indexical nature, always suggesting a whole action by its salient parts, always directing the attention of the spectator by pointing to the incidents most worthy of his attention. Yet theatre is not merely a means of signifying something else; it is not merely a semiotic record of a past action. It is itself an action, a real event in real time. The danger of semiotics is that it distracts our attention from the real experience that lies at the core of performance.

Elements of theatre: fire, light, shadow, performer

Theatre grows from real elemental forces, especially fire and light. Performance is made visible by the fire of the sun, which casts its light on the world. The light strikes objects, casting shadows:

> If we shadows have offended,
> Think but this, and all is mended,
> That you have but slumber'd here
> While these visions did appear.
> And this weak and idle theme
> No more yielding but a dream . . . .
> (*A Midsummer Night's Dream*, v.i.412–17)

Shadow is a term used in Shakespeare's time for actor or performer.

Aeschylus opens his *Oresteia* with a bonfire casting unexpected light through the night. Shakespeare uses the candle (fire-light) as a convention to establish night and as a metaphor encapsulating the equation of world and theatre. Lady Macbeth sleep walks carrying a candle:

> DOCTOR.   How came she by that light?
> GENTLEWOMAN.   Why, it stood by her. She has light by her continually. 'Tis her command.
> DOCTOR.   You see her eyes are open.
> GENTLEWOMAN.   Ay, but their sense is shut.
> (*Macbeth*, v.i.20–4)

Lady Macbeth's open-eyed blindness has turned her from a person into a shadow, whose time on stage is fast drawing to a close. When Macbeth does hear of her death he describes her as a candle, including himself in the image: 'Out, out brief candle / Life's but a walking shadow, a poor player . . .' (v.v.23–4). When Lear's Fool is groping in his mind for an image to describe his sense of cataclysm he says, 'out went the candle and we were left darkling' (*King Lear*, I.iv.216). At the end of *Othello*, Othello conceives of his murder of Desdemona as snuffing a light:

> Put out the light, and then put out the light.
> If I quench thee thou flaming minister,
> I can again thy former light restore,
> Should I repent me; but once put out thy light,
> Thou cunning'st pattern of excelling nature,
> I know not where is that Promethean heat
> That can thy light relume.
>
> (v.ii.7–12)

While the shadow's light can be relumed, Desdemona's cannot.

This is not unlike the old Anglo-Saxon view of life. According to Bede, when King Edwin was debating with his counsellors about the new doctrine of Christianity, one of them offered him a most powerful metaphor of fire and air:

> Your majesty, when we compare the present life of man on earth with that time of which we have no knowledge, it seems to me like the swift flight of a single sparrow through the banqueting hall where you are sitting at dinner on a winter's day with your thanes and counsellors. In the midst there is a comforting fire to warm the hall, outside, the storms of winter rain or snow are raging. This sparrow flies swiftly in through one door of the hall, and out through another. While he is inside he is safe from the winter storms; but after a few moments of comfort, he vanishes from sight into the wintry world from which he came.[13]

The moments a performer spends on stage, strutting and fretting as Macbeth describes it, seem to me very similar to this description of life. Both in the physical aspect of stepping from the dark into the light and back again, and in the emotional aspect of a sudden burst of intense consciousness, performing is a process of exploring states of being unfamiliar to us in our off-stage lives. We know precious little about where we come from, and less still about where we may be going; but in performance, or watching performers, we sometimes glimpse a higher order of understanding, a higher plane of feeling.

It is the paradoxical nature of theatrical time which makes this possible. When we take part in a performance, as actors or audience, we collude in an exploration of the way in which through performance the past becomes present again. This is what Shakespeare means in Sonnet 15 by the 'war with Time', for, while the passage of time seems merely day by day, minute by minute, to increase the store of what has been, the theatre redresses the balance by reclaiming the past for the present. In this it is like the fire which Edwin's counsellor depicts at the centre of the hall of life, that strangely paradoxical phenomenon so popular with emblematists: fire grows by consuming, and the bigger it becomes the more it decays.

Shakespeare casts the death of his most enigmatic and grand heroine, Cleopatra, in similar terms, exploring still more deeply the paradox of fire:

> Give me my robe, put on my crown; I have
> Immortal longings in me. Now no more
> The juice of Egypt's grape shall moist this lip.
> Yare, yare, good Iras; quick. Methinks I hear
> Antony call. I see him rouse himself
> To praise my noble act. I hear him mock
> The luck of Caesar, which the gods give men
> To excuse their after wrath. Husband I come.
> Now to that name my courage prove my title!
> I am fire and air; my other elements
> I give to baser life.
>   (*Antony and Cleopatra*, v.ii.278–88)

She robes herself for her greatest act – Shakespeare can never resist a pun on act – and her marriage is her death. Her expression of sexual fulfilment and hope for the future, 'Husband I come', is simultaneously the end of her mortal life. Throughout his work, Shakespeare explores the relationship between theatre and the world, but never more forcefully than here, for the fire of inspiration which in traditional Christian thought is deemed to descend from God to man at the moment of sacramental blessing here is shown to come from within a woman, to be the ultimate expression of her humanity.

The choice of fire is obviously not accidental, nor merely a metaphysical indicator of a neo-Platonic value system operating in Cleopatra's mind. It represents at the highest level the sacred power of the spirit, the power of life itself, as Edwin's counsellor so powerfully understood. It is the Promethean power that man stole from the gods and made his own. It is the gift of God to the disciples after the ascension of Jesus.

Perhaps Plato distrusted the theatre because of its elemental affinity with fire, light and shadow, for it is precisely these forces he uses in his own metaphor of the imprisoned imagination:

> I want you to go on to picture the enlightenment or ignorance of our human conditions somewhat as follows. Imagine an underground chamber, like a cave with an entrance open to the daylight and running a long way underground. In this chamber are men who have been prisoners there since they were children, their legs and necks being so fastened that they can only look straight ahead of them and cannot turn their heads. Behind them and above them a fire is burning, and between the fire and the prisoners runs a road, in front of which a curtain wall has been built, like the screen at puppet shows between the operators and their audience . . . do you think our prisoners could see anything of themselves or their fellows except the shadows thrown by the fire on the wall of the cave opposite them?[14]

If the imprisoned imagination is like watching a puppet show, is not the freedom to perform in live theatre a plausible image of the liberated mind, as Shakespeare thought it to be?

Yet there is, as always in theatre, a more mundane and less metaphysically daunting aspect to the metaphor, a correlative in the world of concrete experience. That feeling of warmth we get from enjoying ourselves in the theatre is partly the warmth generated by a large crowd of people gathered in a confined space, partly that experience many of us have had of entering the Christmas pantomime, with its pinks and golds, and its very Europeanised Orient or Middle East, from the wet or frosty street, when we too feel something like the sparrow on its journey in and out of the great, fire-lit hall.

Chapter 3

I Engraft You New: Learning to Perform

We learn performance techniques in three main ways: *playing*, *rehearsing* and *performing*. Each of these relates to an aspect of development of the performance self:

1 *Playing*: learning to express the self
2 *Rehearsing*: learning to express the 'self' of another – creating a role
3 *Performing*: the interaction of expressed self with other selves

Seen as a dialectic, playing concerns being, rehearsing representing, and performance is the synthesis of the two. All three stages of this dialectic take place in the context of group work, whether in (1) the classroom or playground, (2) the rehearsal studio, or (3) the theatre. This chapter will deal with the first two categories, the remainder of the book the third.

Playing: learning to express the self

Although performers have to acquire special skills in learning how to inhabit consciousnesses other than their own, they share with non-performers the need to learn about their own bodies and minds. Humanist education systems have traditionally valued theatre as a means of teaching and learning such self-awareness, even treating the discipline of teaching itself as analogous to performance. So learning in general is a natural starting-point for learning how to perform.

Educational and developmental psychology distinguishes between three distinct but interconnected levels of learning self-expression: *psycho-motoric, affective* and *cognitive*. Like anyone else, performers learn at, and operate on, these three levels simultaneously.

Psycho-motoric skills are given the lowest intellectual priority because they are the most 'animal', those concerned with the brain's control and co-ordination of muscular activity. *Gross motor skills*, such as crawling and walking, are acquired first, followed by *fine motor skills*, such as the co-ordination of the eye and the hand, which allows us to compute distances and hence pick up implements. Of greatest complexity are the fine motor skills required in articulating sounds: the control of breathing, vocal chords, larynx, tongue, jaw and lips.

Affective skills tend to be treated next in order of significance and have to do with the expression of emotions and feelings. We learn by observation and imitation how to develop from the relatively unsophisticated, though highly powerful, affective skills of crying and laughing to a complex language of emotional signals. We learn, too, that there are certain culturally determined conventions as to how emotions are expressed, and that our success in conveying those emotions may depend as much on our ability to find the correct conventions of expression as on the sincerity with which we feel them. Behind this relatively well understood 'body language', however, lies a *micro-gestural* system, in which the finest details of muscular movement convey signals about state of mind and mood. Relatively little is yet known about how this system works, partly because it is so complex in nature: the face alone has a vast range of possible muscular configurations, each of which potentially carries affective meaning. But it is likely that, the further research proceeds, the more a performer's power of expression will be related to mastery of micro-gesture, as developed in rehearsal.[1]

Cognitive skills tend to be given the highest priority in learning since they refer to those abilities that are held to distinguish man from all other animals. All animate creatures have systems of communication, and many are capable of generating wide varieties of sounds, but man alone has the cognitive ability to develop spoken language and complex numerical notation. Man has also developed successful expedients for enhancing and extending his memory, and hence his knowledge: writing, print and now digitised information storage enable him to store infinitely more information than an individual memory could store, and reading enables him to access that information at will. The performer draws on these skills and his memory in order to read, learn and then reproduce his part.

Performance, as an integrative discipline, challenges the hierarchy of psycho-motoric, affective and cognitive skills, because in the enactment of a scene all three are in use simultaneously. Cognitive acting with affect generates 'words, mere words, no matter from the heart'; affective acting produces bombastic and lachrymose sounds signifying nothing; and, without psycho-motoric control, neither can occur in the first place.

Learning as adaptation

As Jean Piaget[2] and the developmental psychologists who have advanced his work have shown, the reasons why we acquire the skills of movement and speech are largely pragmatic: we feel need or discomfort and signal that need or discomfort to those around us. If our signals bring the desired effect, then gradually we commit to memory more and more economical ways of achieving the desired end. In all learning the principle of economy or effort is dominant. Progress is necessarily slow, both because the processes we go through to acquire skills such as speech are extremely complex – still, in fact, beyond our comprehension – and because learning can only proceed at a moderate pace. Until we have mastered simple procedures, we cannot proceed to complex ones, and, if demands are made on us, or skills taught to us far beyond our current executive capacity, we simply block them out or forget them. This gives rise to the psychological principle of *moderate innovation*,[3] a principle which states that learning is a linear, evolutionary process that can only proceed at a certain, moderate speed.

In Piaget's terms,[4] our first learning-steps concern the acquisiton of *schemes*. Schemes are the basic units of our behaviour, analogous to words in language. They may be partly inherent in our genetic or biological make-up, partly acquired through interaction with our environment. Human anatomy and physiology set limits to what we can do with our bodies, yet within these limits there are wide variations in the skills of particular individuals. The question of whether what we achieve is entirely predetermined by our *nature* or by a function of our *nurture*, or is a product of both, is not one I wish to sidetrack into, other than to suggest that the performing artist by his very existence seems to me to contradict the hard-line *nature* argument which allows for no intervention of the individual will in the acquisition and execution of human schemes. What does matter to my argument is that the learning-process as described by Piaget is a dialectical one, one that in a radically condensed form is the basis of rehearsal. Rehearsal, like learning, is premissed on what Piaget describes as *adaptation*.

If behavioural schemes are analogous to individual words in a vocabulary, we soon learn to combine schemes into more complex *organisations*, the behavioural equivalent to verbal *utterances*. Organisations enable us to achieve simultaneous or complex objectives, such as not being fed when we feel hungry, but being fed what we should like to eat, in the correct amounts and at the desired temperature. In the early months, we acquire schemes and organisations more by observation and imitation – trial and error – than by inventiveness of our own. This process is called *assimilation*. But, as we develop individual and differentiated consciousness, we begin to personalise what we are learning, changing schemes and organisations to our own purposes. This is known as *accommodation*, the alteration of existing, and invention of new modes of expression. In stage terms, learning one's lines may be understood as a process of assimilation, learning how to interpret and play them, one of accommodation.

Thresholds of learning

In the most radical moments of accommodation, we pass through *thresholds* of experience and consciousness. These are central in drama because they appear to break the developmental principle of moderate innovation and thus set problems of identity and recognition for which there are no immediate solutions. It is through such a threshold that Oedipus passes when being told who he really is, or Macbeth, when shown his future by the Weird Sisters. It is the threshold of the known that Dr Faustus commits his life, and soul, to exploring, and he loses both when he crosses the threshold of human knowledge into the ineffable. For the performer the psychological concept of the threshold is fundamental, in that until he has crossed the threshold of another consciousness – the consciousness of the role to be played – he cannot hope to convey it to an audience.

Learning to play: imitation, pleasure, discipline

The most casual observation of children at play shows how much role play is part of their learning-process. Whether the game is 'mothers and fathers', 'princes and princesses', 'doctors and nurses' or just 'gangs', imaginative construction of a possible world is the core of the activity. Even playing on their own, children will assume roles, often holding conversations between a number of assumed characters or articulating the feelings and words of several dolls at once. Some connection must exist, therefore, between children's play and theatrical performance, but this connection is not a straightforward one.

Aristotles theory of tragedy as 'the imitation of an action' has one of its roots in a general theory of the relationship between imitation and learning:

> Poetry in general seems to have sprung from two causes, each of them lying deep in our nature. First, the instinct of imitation is implanted in man from childhood, one difference between him and other animals being that he is the most imitative of living creatures, and through imitation learns his earliest lessons; and no less universal is the pleasure felt in things imitated.[5]

The implication of Aristotle's position is that the child's predisposition to play and imitate leads inevitably to theatrical performance, but there are too many cultures in which no such linear evolution has occurred to allow us to accept his generalisation. Indeed, classical Athenian culture is the exception rather than the rule in early European history in having generated a high-status theatrical culture at all.

Where Aristotle is unequivocally right is in the identification of pleasure in imitation, or indeed sheer pleasure, as a powerful force in learning. Lord Bacon was aware, if suspicious, of this pleasure principle, as were the Jesuits. But he recognised that theatre was not solely about pleasure, demanding simultaneously discipline of a kind vital to the enhancement of the individual's powers of expression:

> It also deserves to be remarked, that even ordinary talents in great men, used on occasions, may sometimes produce remarkable effects. And of this we will give an eminent instance, the rather because the Jesuits judiciously retain the discipline among them. And though the thing itself be disreputable in the profession of it, yet it is excellent as a discipline: we mean the action of the theatre, which strengthens the memory, regulates the tone of the voice, and the efficacy of pronunciation; gracefully composes the countenance and the gesture; procures a coming degree of assurance; and lastly accustoms youth to the eyes of men.[6]

Bacon defends performance on two levels which relate directly to the threefold learning-model I have outlined: it encourages children to develop the skills of speech and gesture, so teaching both psycho-motoric co-ordination and affective use of the body and the voice; it also trains the memory and gives confidence and articulacy, which enhances cognitive development. This blend of pleasure and discipline was later to be seen by Herbert Marcuse as the basis of culture itself, a product of the dialectic of the short-term, gratificatory *pleasure principle* and the longer-term, disciplined *reality principle*.[7]

Schiller puts a different emphasis on the concept of play and its relationship with human performance. In his 'letters' *On the Aesthetic Education of Man*, he identifies in man three basic manifestations of the will: the 'will to form' (*Formtrieb*), the 'will to content' (*Stofftrieb*), and the integrative 'will to play' (*Spieltrieb*). Out of the dialectic of form and content equivalent to the dialectic of the actant and his performing space, emerges a new will, that which transcends both form and content in free, wholly improvised expression. Schiller's case rests on two principles: first, that to be is to play; secondly, that 'play' in its aesthetic sense is the highest manifestation of the human spirit.[8]

The first principle is expressed like this: 'a man only plays when he is, in the fullest sense of the word, a man, and *he is only fully a man when he plays*' (Letter 15).[9] The second, which illuminates the apparent tautology of the first, makes a connection between play and aesthetic freedom: 'From this play of *free association of ideas*, which at first is of an entirely material kind and which may be explained entirely according to natural laws, the imagination finally, in the attempt at *a free form*, makes the leap to aesthetic play' (Letter 27).[10] Schiller describes the means by which, through the master of form and content, the restrictive, rule-bound nature of play suddenly makes a leap into the spontaneous, the improvised.

At a mundane level, this expresses no more than our everyday experience. We all learn the principles of articulacy in an empirical way, however much we may benefit from prescriptive analysis of such skills. But, at a metaphysical level, the point Schiller is making is that only through mastery of rules and conventions is freedom possible. The disciplined rehearsal process enables the freedom of performance, and all performance, even of classic texts, tends to the 'free form' of improvisation.

Rehearsal: learning to express the self of another

As I suggested in Chapter 2, the cultural process of performance rests ultimately on a shared consciousness of performance conventions. It is this consciousness which most markedly distinguishes the 'playing' conducted in rehearsal and the children's playing described above. The steps towards such consciousness, however, mirror the processes of assimilation and accommodation in learning as a whole.

Rehearsal has two interconnected but distinct purposes: administrative (assimilatory) and interpretative (accommodatory). First, the rehearsal schedule is designed administratively to ensure that performers learn their parts, know when to come on and when to leave, and where entries and exits are to be made. Secondly, interpretatively, rehearsal offers time for exploration of the character and characteristics of the role to be played, both in itself, and in relationships with other characters and the development of an artistic concept for the performance as a whole.

Brecht sees the acting-process as an assimilatory one of *observation*:

You, the actor
Must above all other arts
Master the art of observation.

Important is not what you look like, therefore, but
What you have seen and show. Worth knowing
Is what you know.
People will observe you to see
How well you have observed.

A different point, akin to Rousseau's view of celebration as an
enabler of community, is made a little later in the same work:

The art of observation
Applied to mankind, is but a branch of the
Art of handling people. Your task, actor, is
To be researcher and teacher in the art of handling people.
Knowing their nature and showing it, you teach them
To handle themselves. You teach them the great art
Of living together.[11]

Brecht, like Shakespeare, treats theatre as a metaphor of the world,
even if his world view differs in some respects from Shakespeare's.
But his theory has one weakness when viewed in the context of
Piaget's work. By emphasising so heavily the assimilatory
observation of others, Brecht risks excluding the need for
accommodatory observation and adaptation of the self.

Administration and procedures

The procedures of rehearsal are similar to those of any assimilation
process, depending heavily on discipline and repetition. First, the
'timetable' is determined by the agreed hours of work, known as the
rehearsal schedule or *call sheet*. Secondly, it is premissed on the
empirical observation that learning complex statements takes time.
Traditionally, rehearsals fall into three-hour blocks, the working
day being, therefore, two three-hour rehearsals. Each rehearsal is
known as a *call*. The current average rehearsal time for repertory is
three weeks, or ninety rehearsal hours. Such averages are,
however, susceptible to relatively rapid change. Ellen Terry
thought Irving highly demanding in insisting on one week of
rehearsal. Peter Stein, the contemporary German director, thinks
nothing of spending months in rehearsal and even more time in
pre-rehearsal preparation.

Parallel to these periods of work for the performers are the technical and building programmes, run by the *technical director*. These intersect with the rehearsal schedule for costume and technical calls, but will often have been initiated long in advance of rehearsal in discussions between the *director*, who has overall control of the artistic aspects of performance and the *designer*, whose responsibility is for the way the performance and the performers look. The designer will issue instructions to the *scene shop*, where set and props are made, and to the *wardrobe* for costumes. If the performance is dance-based, or contains dance, the director will be replaced, or assisted, by a *choreographer*. Music will be controlled by a *conductor* or a *musical director*. Regrettably few productions can afford a *voice coach*, someone whose task it is to ensure that performers are making optimum use of their vocal abilities.

Just prior to performance in front of an audience comes the *dress* or *general* rehearsal. In charge of the administration of rehearsal times will be the *stage-manager*, whose job is to ensure punctuality in rehearsal and a smooth-running performance.

Financing and selling the production will be the responsibility of the theatre management, or the *producer*. He will take charge of contractual negotiations with performers whom the director may have cast, oversee the *production budget* and the *box office*, where the tickets are sold. Overall artistic policy may well be considerably influenced by the producer because of his financial authority, although formally this will be the responsibility of the *artistic director*. The production budget may directly determine the length of rehearsal time allowed.

Interpretation

While the ultimate purpose of rehearsal may be to realise a particular, probably directorial, view of the meaning of a given play, its daily shape will be more directly determined by the need for disciplined work, regular and demanding repetition, detailed personal exploration and group negotiation. Fatigue is commonly a greater enemy than lack of invention, and a successful director will be asked to demonstrate a talent for leadership and psychological understanding every bit as much as artistic inspiration.

The performer needs to know how the person he is portraying

may move, how his voice may sound, what affective behaviour he is likely to show, and how his mind works. It is common for performers to find a way into the consciousness of another first by finding the appropriate way to move, then by developing some typical behavioural mannerisms, and finally by working out a means of representing his patterns of thought and his attitudes. Equally common is the experience that moving a part in rehearsal makes line-learning easier: this is partly because the sequence of movements facilitates the acquisition of a sequence of words, partly because movement of a rehearsed kind trigger the verbal memory. In this, actors are no different from children, who find action songs easier to memorise than narrative ballads because they integrate words and actions.

Any higher level of directorial interpretation must grow out of the action-learning process, which it is the director's task to co-ordinate and lead. This makes the director's task a combination of highway codesman ensuring that 'the two hours traffic of the stage' flows freely, and Hamlet's famous 'mirror up to nature', the glass into which the performers look to discover what effect they are having. In that sense, the director functions as audience, stimulating the 'audience' component of the performer's self to a point where the performer no longer needs the external monitor.

Conventions of notation

In rehearsal many complex decisions about how to perform are made in a relatively short time; these decisions are recorded in the *prompt book*, which acts as the memory of the production, using notational devices as a shorthand of the conclusions reached. Repertory theatres in particular rely heavily on such books, especially when a show is revived by someone other than the original director.

There are three co-ordinates for any stage movement, representing the position of the performer in relation to the height, depth and width of the performance space. The outer dimensions of the performance space will determine the practical limits within which a given movement can take place, but it is also a favourite trick of theatre to deceive the eye, and have performers appear to walk through walls, or sink into the floor. This is one practical way in which spatial dimensions are relativised. The practical constraint on movement is the relative inability of the human performer to work in the vertical plane. He can bend over, jump and stretch up, but, short of being lifted on a harness like Peter Pan, the only way to gain height is to go up stairs, or stand on a balcony or battlements. One of Max Reinhardt's trademarks as a director was the use of steps or stairs, and this way he was able to get much more variety into the vertical movements he could ask of his actors.

The conventions of describing where a performer is at any point in a scene are determined by a notional symmetrical grid laid over the stage area. Left (L) and right (R) on this grid are the performer's, not the audience's, so, because the performer tends, at least in the picture-frame theatre, to be facing the audience, *stage left* (SL) is the audience's right and *stage right* (SR) the audience's left. When a performer moves towards the audience he moves *down-stage* (D), and when he moves away he moves *up-stage* (U). The stage area within the proscenium is the *main stage*, and that which butts out from it the *forestage* or, if somewhat larger, the *thrust*. A performer may enter *down-stage left* (DL), or *down-stage right* (DR), i.e. near the audience; *centre-stage left* (CL), or *centre-stage right* (CR), half-way back; or *up-stage right* (UR), *left* (UL) or *centre* (UC), i.e. from the back as the audience sees it. When on the performance area, he moves up- or down-stage, and stage right or stage left if he is moving across. Diagonals are simply referred to as such.

The stage area is divided into an invisible, geometric grid, whose co-ordinates are set by number and position of points of access to it; these are sometimes, as in large nineteenth-century proscenium-arch theatres, as many as twelve – four on each side and four at the back. These were supplemented by occasional entries through floor traps, trick wall flats and from the fly-tower.

In classical, thrust-stage or proscenium-arch theatre the strongest move a performer can make is from up-stage centre (the middle of the back wall) straight down-stage to the front. The powerful closing sequence of the musical *Hair* consisted of a long chorus advance down-stage, ending up at full volume on the very edge of the stage. The strongest exit is the reverse. The weakest movements are across the stage: in *Oedipus*, for example, Oedipus's power is directly expressed when he emerges out of huge central doors, symbolising the palace, while the Chorus files in from the side of the stage to meet him. Oedipus's fall is graphically registered by his final exit to the side of the stage. The dramatic death of the murderer Robert Macaire – one of Irving's favourite roles – has him slumped over a bridge in the very centre of the proscenium picture, frozen in a tableau of retribution.

Partly because they are technically harder to effect, partly because they are not easily recognisable within naturalistic conventions, entries, exits and moves in the vertical dimension tend to carry special, often religious or moral, significance. Don Juan goes down into Hell; in *Hamlet*, the Ghost speaks from under the stage, and Hamlet, half-way to death, leaps into Ophelia's grave. By contrast, neo-classical deities descend on clouds to bring Baroque masques and operas to a close, and saints and martyrs are carried up through the firmament to a place of eternal glory. In *Peter Pan*, Peter's special powers are signalled by the fact that he can move in the vertical plane and allow others to do the same. In Peter Brook's *A Midsummer Night's Dream*, Brook cunningly played on the associations of movement in the vertical plane to give genuinely magical powers to his fairies.

Partly to counteract this problem, partly for reasons of perspective, large stages tend to be *raked* – set at an angle – and use raised sections to vary the vertical dimensions. Productions of Wagner's *Ring*, such as Hans Hotter's at Covent Garden and Patrice Chéreau's at Bayreuth, have made visually exciting use of the vertical plane, Hotter staging the operas on a large, mobile ring, and Chéreau setting much of the action on and around a hydroelectric dam.

Two factors complicate the neat logic of horizontal stage co-ordinates. The first is that the stage thus described has two potential centres of power, depending on which theatrical convention is held to be operating. The *naturalistic* convention is premissed on the belief that the performers, to achieve the illusion of authenticity, behave as if they were in real space, the audience looking at them through an invisible *fourth wall*. In such a room, the centre of power is the physical centre of the set, the bisection point of the two diagonals. The second convention, the *meta-theatrical*, works on the opposite premiss, that the whole point of theatre is that it should declare itself to be a performance art, an art of show. By the terms of this convention, the audience's space is the complementary half of the performers, which makes the most powerful place on stage the middle of the front of the stage, which is the bisection point of the diagonals of the whole space.

The tension that exists between these two possible centres is accentuated by a second factor, that the space may not be arranged in a rectilinear fashion at all. Most proscenium-arch theatres seat their audiences in curved rows, for better sight lines and better acoustics. This curve implies a complementary opposite curve on stage: if a performer wishes to cross the stage remaining the same distance from the audience to achieve the illusion of walking straight, he in fact has to describe a curve. In the context of Rousseau's observations about performance space being in prototype curvilinear, this points to a more radical dialectic in the space than the clash of centres described above. For now at issue is whether the space is organised in terms of the inclusive circle or in terms of the exclusive frame. One's consciousness as a performer will be decisively influenced by whether one's movement is intended to include the audience in a group feeling and group expression, or the reverse.

Rehearsing moves

It is at the levels of learning how to move and speak in role that the adaptory nature of rehearsal is most visible. First, moves and lines have to be assimilated. Then through rehearsal the performer accommodates the role, so that, by the time he comes to perform, its schemes and organisations appear to be naturally and spontaneously his own.

Moving convincingly as another depends on subsuming into one's own unconscious the habits of movement proper to one's role. Success in this depends in turn on the extent to which one is conscious of how movement is an index of the self. Acquiring this generic consciousness of movement, or what Rudolf Laban calls *awareness*, is of greater significance than the detail of how to describe specific moves. (Readers who wish to acquire a notational system for movement are here referred to Laban's, which is as good as any in current use.[12]) It means knowing how to control the speed, force and duration of a movement, and to correlate movement to feeling and to action. At one level of sophistication this will mean the ability to juggle, stage-fight, tumble or dance. At another, it will mean the ability to represent widely varying emotions convincingly to an audience.

Brecht wrote one of the classic scenes in which the relationship between character and movement is explored, when Arturo Ui is taught how to move in a dictatorial way by an out-of-work Shakespearian actor:

UI.   Walk around like they do in Shakespeare.

The ACTOR *walks around.*

UI.   Good.
GIVOLA   But you can't appear in front of the Cauliflower Trust like that! It's not natural!
UI.   What do you mean, not natural? Nobody is natural today. When I walk, I wish it to be noticed that I am walking.

He copies the ACTOR'S *gait.*

ACTOR.   Head back. (UI *tilts his head back*.) The foot contacts the ground first with the point. (UI *touches the ground first with the point of his foot*.) Good. Excellent. You are a natural. Now we must just do something about the arms. Stiff. Wait a moment. The best thing would be to cross them in front of your genitals. (UI *crosses his hands in front of his genitals as he walks*.) Not bad. Informal, yet in command. But the head must be back. Right.   (*Arturo Ui*, vi)[13]

The scene shows how all three levels of movemental learning – psycho-motoric, affective and cognitive – have to be integrated in order to produce convincing movements, and at the same time how power and authority can be rehearsed.

Laban describes the structured and conscious movement of dance in linguistic terms:

It is a language of action in which the various intentions and bodily and mental efforts of man are arranged in coherent order. . . . Dancing can be understood as an attempt to assimilate the rules of the fluent co-ordination of the operation of body and mind through the practical experience of the many combinations of its constituents.[14]

At a simple level, we may construct a distinction between *move-*

ment and *moves*, equivalent to the distinction in linguistics between *langue* and *parole*. By *langue* is meant the potential, or negative capability, of a given language, a notional measure of all that it could express. By *parole* is meant individual acts of expression, or *utterances*. *Movement* may be understood as the negative capability of bodily expression, a description of all that could be done. *Moves*, which include *gestures*, are the expressive units, the movemental equivalent to the utterance.

There are three main forces acting upon us when we learn the language of movement: a practical, psycho-motoric need to be co-ordinated in order to move unaided, feed ourselves and protect ourselves from danger; an affective need to express our feelings through, and with the aid of, articulate movement; and a cognitive need to use our ability to determine how we move to convey opinions and information.

Laban identifies sixteen steps towards learning how to move:

1 Awareness of the body
2 Awareness of weight and time
3 Awareness of space
4 Awareness of the flow of the body weight in space and time
5 Adaptation to the partner
6 Instrumental use of the body
7 Awareness of isolated actions
8 Occupational rhythms
9 The shape of movement
10 Exploring effort actions
11 Orientation in space
12 Shape and effort involving separate parts of the body
13 Elevation from the ground
14 Group feeling
15 Group formation
16 Expressive quality

Valuable though all the headings are, the list has no obvious sequential logic to it.

The way the Actor teaches Arturo Ui to walk and to stand is perhaps a good point at which to approach a revision of Laban's list. While it is Ui's awareness that by walking differently he may be able to appear more authoritative, the Actor teaching him proceeds from the opposite position, that only when he has learned to walk in an authoritative way can he begin to think about being more powerful. Thus the awareness of the pupil that change is possible is a necessary precondition for change, but change itself is led from the practical rather than the theoretical point of view.

The steps Ui goes through are:

1 Awareness of existing role
2 Awareness of the need to change role
3 Awareness of the connection between movement and role
4 Awareness of movement as relative and changeable
5 Decision to change role through movement
6 Employment of teacher to teach movement and role

In practice this reflects itself in the following phases of activity:

1 Observation of potential role models
2 Selection of desired role model
3 Imitation of role model with practical instruction in isolated actions, according to the principles of weight, space, time, elevation above the ground and the shape of movement
4 Imitation of role model in sequential and complex action (flow)
5 Reorientation within space
6 Assimilation of role model into consciousness
7 Observation of effect of new role on partner
8 Accommodation of self to partner's response to role
9 Exploitation of new role model

The steps the Actor goes through are

1 Acceptance of commission to teach
2 Orientation within strange space
3 Observation and analysis of pupil's needs
4 Demonstration of role model as isolated actions, according to the principles of weight, space, time, elevation above the ground and the shape of movement, with explanation
5 Observation and criticism of detail
6 Relationship of practical detail to pupil's purpose and capability
7 Demonstration of role model in sequential and complex action
8 Judgement of overall effect

In order to communicate so quickly they must share:

1 Awareness of their own bodies
2 Awareness of the partner's body
3 Adaptability to the partner
4 Awareness of the body as occupational tool (acting/politics)
5 Awareness of the body as gestural instrument (making speeches)
6 Common perceptions of expressive quality
7 Common value systems *vis à vis* Givola's objections

It is the last category, of common value systems, to which the pursuit of awareness, or consciousness, is ultimately directed.

Rehearsing roles: finding voices

The complementary part of the scene in which Ui learns to move is the section in which he learns to speak, the Actor choosing for him the role model Mark Antony, an irony lost on Ui. In the Forum speech, Ui finds a new voice and that voice determines his new character. This relationship between character and voice is one Shakespeare himself explores a good deal, especially in rehearsal scenes in which performers find their way to character through voice.

In *A Midsummer Night's Dream*, i.ii, we see the Mechanicals gathering to rehearse. Peter Quince, director and author, calls the roll and then casts the parts. These constitute a list of stock characters, with set voices:

The lover: draws tears from the audience, moving storms of
    emotion and eliciting sighs of pity
The tyrant: is lofty, raging and strong
The woman: is high-pitched and small-voiced
The lion: roars

Other characters, such as mothers and fathers, need no vocal direction since their role is determined by who they are not by how they speak. Finally, Quince indicates that he will make a list of props, and the first rehearsal ends.

By Act III scene i, rehearsals are in full swing. The space is designated – 'this green plot shall be our stage, this hawthorn brake our tiring house' – and the work begins. First problem on the agenda is the likely response of the ladies to a lion and to swords. So a prologue, explaining that neither the lion nor the swords are real, is agreed: 'Write me a prologue; and let the prologue seem to say we will do no harm with our swords, and that Pyramus is not kill'd indeed.' Even at this level of performance, there is a consciousness of the simultaneity of being and representing. Next more elaborate technical problems are solved, such as the wall and moonshine, before the detailed work of setting out moves and interpreting lines begins. Bottom mistakes 'odorous' for 'odious', and is corrected; then Flute speaks his whole part at once, and is briefly informed about the rules of dialogue. Finally Bottom misses his cue. The rehearsal is disrupted by an unexpected transformation, Bottom's into an ass, which, after their debate about real and imaginary lions, should perhaps frighten the others less than in reality it does. The reason why it is so frightening is that there has been no designatory act to precede the entry. Puck has changed the transformational rules.

In *Hamlet*, ii.ii, Hamlet intervenes in the action both as playwright and director. He changes the script of *The Murder of Gonzago*, which the Players are to perform at court, and performs a heroic speech in a manner that elicits praise from Polonius for its 'good accent and good discretion'. Later, in Act iii scene ii, he tells the performers how to speak their roles: 'Speak the speech I pray you, as I pronounc'd it, trippingly on the tongue. . . . Nor do not saw the air too much with your hand, thus, but use all gently. . . . Suit the action to the word, the word to the action.' The advice is general in character, and depends on too many imponderables, such as what Hamlet means by 'trippingly', to constitute a serious lesson in direction. Rather, Shakespeare may be using the scene to demonstrate how amateurs, such as princes of Denmark, think they know better than professionals how to deliver lines. Nevertheless, Hamlet does show in miniature how the director works, acting out for the performer how he sees role being portrayed, and holding a mirror up to the performer as to how his interpretation might affect an audience.

Character and characteristic

Much of the theatrical repertoire exploits a relatively limited

number of character types in finely shaded variations.
Characterisation is largely understood as a function of specific
combinations of behavioural characteristics associated with role
type. Lovers sigh; lions roar. From the performer's point of view,
this makes the process of rehearsal one first of assimilating the
characteristics of his role type, and then their accommodation into
a plausible portrayal. For example, the seventeenth-century
repertoire of the English Comedians is constructed around the
following role types:

The young lover
The desirable girl
The king/tyrant
The wise father
The shrewish woman
The witty/coarse/acrobatic clown
The prodigal/dupe
Virtue
Vice/devil/necromancer

An individual identity could be achieved by varying combinations
of types, such as young lover and dupe, desirable girl and shrewish
woman, king and vice.

Directly contemporary with the success of the English
Comedians was that of the *commedia dell'arte*, which uses

The young lover
The desirable girl
The father/guardian (Pantalone)
The lawyer (Dottore)
The Zanni (Arlecchino, Pedrolino, Pulcinella, Columbina)

In this case, masks for all except the lovers were a simple way of
establishing exactly which role was which.

Nineteenth-century British theatre uses a similar list:

The lover
The desirable match
The father/guardian
The put-upon wife

The domineering husband
The servant

A relatively small number of background characteristics help determine the execution of role. These are:

Sex: male or female
Age: young or old
Class: high or low
Moral code: good or bad
Kinship status: mother or father, brother or sister, son or daughter, legitimate or illegitimate, married or unmarried
Financial status: rich or poor
Linguistic status: articulate or inarticulate, received standard speech or dialect, verse or prose.

Each of these aspects constitutes a behavioural boundary, the drama emerging from attempts – for example, by young lovers – to breach them in some way.

Genre

Stereotypic conventions of character reinforce stereotypic generic attitudes. Tyrants and heroes appear in tragedies, and they largely end up dead. Lovers and clowns appear in comedies, and they end up married. Within these categories, there are certain class distinctions, such as between comedy, which is aristocratic; farce, which is bourgeois; and the jig, which is low-class bawdy. Tragedy, which is aristocratic, is matched by melodrama, which is bourgeois. History, like tragedy, concerns itself with the aristrocrat, if not by birth then at least by behaviour; pastoral has the aristocrat playing peasant. Such conventions are at the heart of classical theories of genre.

Shakespeare's dominance in the theatrical repertoire stems generically from his refusal to be bound by generic propriety, such that nearly every play seems to contain intimations of every possible theatrical genre. Put another way, Shakespeare's attitude to genre suggests that each play constitutes its own. His practical lead was the basis of a crucial breakthrough in the theory of generic convention made by G. E. Lessing, who, writing about Shakespeare, pointed out that there is no necessary link between genre and class:

> The names of Princes and heroes can add pomp and majesty to a play: but they contribute nothing towards its emotion. The misfortune of those whose conditions are most like our own must, quite naturally, go deepest into our souls; and if we have sympathy with kings it is with them as men and not as kings.[15]

This turns the issue of character back on itself, each character in the stage repertoire being seen as potentially present in the personality of each performer, who is able both to be and represent anyone he chooses because his personality contains in potential everyone it is possible to be. In those terms, the test of successful characterisation is the extent to which the represented role is made congruent with possible or real being. At one level, we may interpret Lessing's remarks as an early example of theatrical republicanism, a refusal to acknowledge any aristocracy other than that of feeling or of the spirit. But, at another level, Lessing is pre-empting any attempt to make performance a question of class rather than individual experience. True, performances may gain power and esteem from the extent to which they embody the experiences of a whole class. But their generic success rests on their individual impact. We weep first for Lear and second for King Lear.

The role of the performer: naturalism and alienation

Informing a performer's attitude to performance will be his perception of what social role is, as a product of historical contingencies and variable environmental forces, or of predetermined historical laws. On the former premiss, he may attempt an empathetic relationship with his role to the extent that all that the role does and feels the performer experiences as his own behaviour. To achieve such empathy he has to have either known and felt at first hand the emotions of the role, or found some personal correlative that creates as close an approximation to those emotions as possible. On the latter premiss, he may disbelieve in empathy, suspecting it as a diversion from historical imperatives, and so tend to a detached, or alienated, stance.

The logic of naturalism emerged under the influence of scientific inquiry, which during the nineteenth century was developing an increasingly precise and detailed set of tools for measuring the physical world. Theatre, it was argued, should respond to the scientific initiative by becoming something like a laboratory of human behaviour, reproducing with exactitude real behaviour on stage. Emotions were not merely to be represented but felt. Chekhov, whose plays were directed by Stanislavski, had frequent cause to complain that in practice this meant performers spending long periods on stage in floods of tears, with no regard for the overall shape of the play.[16]

The supposed opposite is the meta-theatrical style associated with the Russian formalist theory of *defamiliarisation* and Brecht's theory of *alienation*. The logic behind the theory is that to show anything to an audience it has to be removed from its normal context, and hence defamiliarised, or 'made strange'. Only then can both performers and audience see the thing for what it is. The theory emerges from the Marxist–Hegelian concept of *alienation*, which is a historical not a performance concept. Underlying the dynamic of history is the fact that man is alienated, either from God (Hegel) or from the fruits of his labours and from power (Marx). Alienation in the theatre is an aesthetic correlative to economic alienation, a means of showing the historical processes at work behind any human action. Hence Brecht's interest in *Lehrstücke*, teaching-plays, which were designed not to engage the sympathy of an audience, but to educate the audience in political modes of seeing.

In practice, as I have already argued, all theatrical performance emerges from a dialectic of being and representing. The position is perhaps best described by Karl Gutzkow, commenting on Büchner's work. Gutzkow saw in Büchner a pathologist of events, in which the dispassionate observation of causes was matched by extremely passionate representations of effects:

> You seem to want to abandon the art of medicine, a step which, so I hear, will not make your father very pleased. Do not be so unfair on this discipline, since, or so it seems to me, you have it to thank for your particular strength, by which I mean your unusual lack of inhibition, your autopsy I almost want to say, that comes across in everything you write.[17]

Gutzkow sees the energy and lack of inhibition in Büchner's work as a direct consequence of his scientific rigour being mediated through his passionate commitment to truth and social equity.

This is not to deny that there are significant differences of style and purpose between naturalism and meta-theatre, but to emphasise that a consciousness of performing is an irreducible minimum in both. Where Brecht most obviously differs from Stanislavski is not in the method of acting as such, but in what the purpose of acting is, whether it is to be cognitive and didactic, or affective and cathartic.

The rise of directorial power in the later nineteenth century has implications for a different theory of acting advanced by Edward Gordon Craig, which, in the context of emphasising the overall sovereignty of the director, sees the ideal performer as a *super-marionette*,[18] someone who is capable of enacting in precise and perfect detail the directorial will. The opposite of this position was taken by Craig's contemporary, Max Reinhardt, who despite an iron directorial will, practised two central principles:

1 That each work has its own aesthetic demands and cannot be accommodated within a generic or politically rigid framework
2 That performers must exercise their own intelligence while on stage and not merely act as agents of the directorial will

To these two principles, I add one more:

3 That it is the task of the director to create the physical and aesthetic pre-conditions in which the performer can practise his art

Taken together these principles amount to a call for a new theatrical enlightenment, an emancipation of the performer from the tyranny or ideological or directorial despotism. This will succeed only through the performer's exercise of his own practical intelligence.

Chapter 4

Naught but Shows: Towards a New Poetics of Performance (i)

The elements of the stage spectacle may be divided up into four main categories: (1) *set*, (2) *lighting*, (3) *props*, (4) *costume and make-up*. These constitute the *contextual* elements of performances, but they may, under special circumstances, assume the significance of actants.

I have arranged the contextual elements in notional order of ease and flexibility of movement and adjustment. They have in common the characteristic that they are moved by human or mechanical aid rather than move of their own volition. They have no consciousness, and no independent power of choice.

Sets and settings

The classic function of the set is to establish a location. It may do this by neutral devices such as the use of black or coloured background drapes, a cyclorama, or masking-flats, the purpose of which is to hide the back- and off-stage space from the audience's view, without doing any more than establishing the boundaries of the performing-area. It may, however, as has been the tendency for the past three centuries, construct elaborate pictures and locations of detailed historical accuracy, such as the Forum in Rome, or the Cathedral in Canterbury, or the Paris Opera, or even their domestic equivalent, the box-set interior. On occasion the set will have special functions, allowing effects such as sudden appearances or disappearances to take place. But the literal aspects of set are at best half the issue, for what compliments the physical set is the imaginary *setting*, which is the place the audience is asked to imagine for the action. Properly used, set will be in a synecdochic relationship with setting.

The bare stage of the Elizabethan theatre was simultaneously set and setting. It used the power of negative capability to be both concretely and imaginatively anywhere. Shakespeare gives his audience instructions how to generate settings in the mind:

> Play with your fancies; and in them behold
> Upon the hempen tackle ship-boys climbing;
> Hear the shrill whistle which doth order give
> To sounds confus'd; behold the threaden sails,
> Borne with th'invisible and creeping wind,
> Draw the huge bottoms through the furrowed sea,
> Breasting the lofty surge.
>   (*Henry V*, III, Prologue, 7–13)

Where on film we would now have an establishing shot, showing all this activity, Shakespeare saves time and money by asking us to picture it for ourselves. Rarely is there any need in Shakespeare for a set, the internal architecture of the Globe offering all the essential facilities for performance. Most of the action takes place on the main stage, but scenes requiring height, such as the balcony scene in *Romeo and Juliet* or Richard's descent to the base court in *Richard II*, can be staged using the theatre's own balcony.

Shakespeare explores the relationship between set and setting in *A Midsummer Night's Dream*. The Mechanicals are worried that their courtly audience might not follow the plot of their play if there are no evident naturalistic set conventions, and so they run up against the problem of needing to represent a wall between Pyramus's and Thisbe's house:

QUINCE.   Then there is another thing: we must have a wall in the great chamber; for Pyramus and Thisby, says the story, did talk through the chink of a wall.
SNOUT.   You can never bring in a wall. What say you, Bottom?
BOTTOM.   Some man or other must present Wall; and let him

> have some plaster, or some loam, or some rough cast about him
> to signify wall; and let him hold his fingers thus, and through
> that cranny shall Pyramus and Thisby whisper.   (III.i.55–63)

So the Gordian knot is untied. A man becomes a wall. This
example, and the solution the Mechanicals offer to the problem of
moonshine, which is (a) to open the casement window to allow the
real moon to shine in, and (b) to bring in a man to represent the
moon, makes explicit the extent to which Shakespeare used the
simultaneous power of theatre to be and to represent to achieve a
blend of reality and imagination in his audience's minds. At the
same time, it points to the falsity of the boundary I have drawn
between space and actant, for in this case the set has become an
actant. Indeed, it is probably the best test of a set's functional value
to ask whether it has achieved integration into the performance or
not, for, if not, it was not worth having.

At the opposite end of the spectrum to the setting constructed in
the mind is the elaborately detailed and historically accurate
naturalistic set, in which there is luggage in suitcases, and clothes in
drawers that are never opened nor even referred to. Typical of this
style is:

> VOYNITSKY'S *room: it is his bedroom and also his office. In the*
> *window there is a big table covered with account books and*
> *papers of all sorts; a bureau, bookcases, scales. A smaller table,*
> *for* ASTROV; *on that table there are paints and drawing materials,*
> *beside it a big portfolio. A cage with a starling in it. On the wall a*
> *map of Africa, obviously no use to anyone. A big sofa covered*
> *with American leather. To the left a door leading to other*
> *apartments. On the right a door into the hall; near door, on*
> *right, there is a doormat, that the peasants may not muddy the*
> *floor. An autumn evening. Stillness.*   (*Uncle Vanya*, IV)[1]

The irony of this naturalistic view of set is that it emerged out of a
highly laudable desire to make the stage a place of more serious and
authentic reflection on the human condition than it had recently
been. But its aesthetic effect is to preclude rather than enhance
imaginative intervention by the audience.

The Shakespearian position thus constitutes one end of the
spectrum of attitudes about set; the highly naturalistic conventions
of nineteenth-century theatre, which have now fed into film, the

other. The one sees the imagination of the audience, and hence
setting, as paramount; the other demands a set to be a speaking
picture, persuasive through visual accuracy and environmental
authenticity. There is no absolute answer to the question of which is
better suited to theatre's needs. Different types of play have been
written for different types of theatrical convention. In the broad
sweep of theatre history, the triumph of the scenic painter and
stage-manager from the mid seventeenth century onwards, lasting
well into the present, may turn out to have been a necessary if blind
alley – necessary because what was really being pursued was the
aesthetic of moving pictures, film.

Within the terms of the theatre, however, the triumph of the
scenic designer tended to be at the expense of the performer, as Ben
Jonson in his famous battle with Inigo Jones sensed it would be.[2]
The purpose of rehearsal, as far as it affected the performer, was
more to shoe-horn him into the elaborate machinery of the staged
pictures than to instruct him in his role. The deployment of the
scenic and architectural skills of perspective, while enhancing the
visual quality of the staged picture, restricted the performer's
movements to a narrow corridor at the front of the stage space, for,
if he moved too far towards the back of the set, the perspective trick
became grotesquely distorted by his own misproportion. In this
context, Walter Benjamin's emancipatory appeal to theatre to
resemble no longer Shakespeare's world stage but rather an
exhibition hall seems like an unconscious return to the very
bondage from which epic theatre was trying to escape.[3]

There is some irony in what then happened: as sets and designs
became more elaborate and unwieldy, designers realised that they
were losing the precious capacity of theatrical space to be either
informal or semi-fixed. More, and more elaborate, scenery meant
less and less flexibility and mobility. So a way out was sought in
architectural and mechanical contrivance: fly-towers, traps, stage
hydraulics, treadmills, revolving stages and stage trucks were all
called to the aid of the designer, who in the end could still not
imitate or match the flexibility or inventiveness of the individual
imagination.

With the advent of electrical power it became easier to move the
mechanical elements of the staged picture. Almost simultaneously
it became possible to make sequences of pictures move on film.
Audiences whose taste was primarily for moving, and later talking,
pictures could now go to the cinema instead of the theatre; and as

the secrets of montage and superimposition began to be unveiled so the pictorial imagination could be fully satisfied in the 'picture house'. In the wake of these changes, theatre made a conceptual and practical breakthrough of very considerable importance. Designers such as Adolph Appia and Edward Gordon Craig recognised that what was missing from even the Shakespearian riches of setting was the potential for abstraction – the environment, whether real or imagined, that did not depend essentially on being thought of, or seen to be, a real place.[4] True, Shakespeare suggests such a place in the dream-like world of the Athenian wood; but the breakthrough Appia and Craig made was to understand that set need not be an establisher of location at all, but might be a visual counterpoint to the stage action, a dramatic place. Thus in the move towards greater abstraction there was suddenly more awareness of space as space, and an attempt to embody in set some of the negative capability of setting. Abstraction became a means of mediating between the two.

The principal agent of this change was the new electric stage lighting, which helped transform the cumbersome and dangerous candle- and gas-powered lighting on which theatre had hitherto depended into the highly flexible and safe facility we now have. With the help of electricity the plasticity of the three-dimensional performance space could be exploited to an extent never before possible. Lights could be precisely directed, focused, coloured and varied in intensity. Spatial divisions could be created at the touch of a button and without the expense or difficulty of solid structures. Designers began to exploit the relationship between lit and unlit space, between highlights and shadows and between varying tonal configurations. This did not come overnight; but it was Craig's and Appia's achievement to identify so quickly how powerful a tool lighting was. Taken to its logical conclusion it became the actant in *son et lumière* shows. It also rapidly attracted the critical attention of Brecht, who, worried at the inordinate skill that lighting-designers were beginning to display with their electric palettes, argued for nothing but pure white light in theatre.

Hierarchy and status

With the recognition of the extent to which the set and the setting of a play could in themselves constitute a direct part of the drama of a performance came a growing awareness of the rules of spatial composition, and of the way space can be used as an index of hierarchy and status. Even the smallest of movements on stage is expected by an audience to have significance, and a transparent system of locationary and spatial use and value is an economical and effective means of telling an audience how to understand the relationships between characters.

Theatre has always exploited such rules because public behaviour as a whole is substantially determined by and reflected in them. The classical Greek theatre had elements of scenery, the *periaktoi*, on which were depicted three classic environments, with an innate hierarchy: the court, the city and the pastoral scene. The court was the seat of power and aristocracy, the city the seat of trade and the merchants, and the pastoral world had a dual function of rusticity and aristocratic idyll. A move from the court to the city was a loss of power, and in the albeit idealised world of pastoral there was a basic equality, often represented as the equality of death.

In Shakespeare's theatre a similar threefold division is evident, between the two man-made environments of courts and cities, and the unaccommodated world of nature. Commonly a problem originates in the court or the city and is resolved in the world of nature. In the comedies, the resolution takes place in a rather frightening or cold pastoral world, such as the wood in *A Midsummer Night's Dream* or the world of Arden in *As You Like It*. In the tragedies, the natural forces are wilder and more damaging, as the stormy heath in *King Lear*, or the moving wood in *Macbeth*.

The counterpoint of man-made and natural environments expresses itself in many ways in the theatre. At the primary level there is a dialectic of the rectilinearity of man-made space and the curvilinearity of natural shapes, which is reflected in the interior design of the theatre, with its arcs of seats facing a rectilinear box. This dialectic of straight and curved lines faces man in his attempt to define his place within space altogether, as is symbolically depicted in Leonardo da Vinci's famous cartoon of a man caught equally within a circle and a square. Rousseau's model of a celebratory circle within a town square uses an equivalent spatial dialectic to express the sociological and political alternatives we face. This dialectic is therefore the practical and metaphysical foundation of stage movement.

Few environments are either purely man-made or purely natural, not least because man-made environments are often constructed of natural materials. But at their extremes, they exhibit certain qualitative differences which may be described as follows:

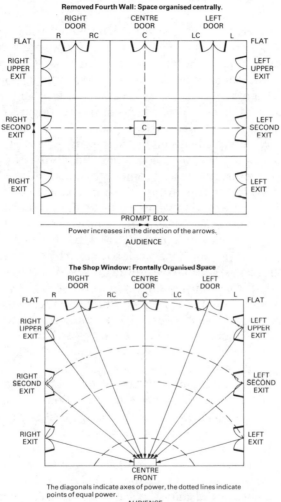

Removed Fourth Wall: Space organised centrally.

Power increases in the direction of the arrows.
AUDIENCE

The Shop Window: Frontally Organised Space

The diagonals indicate axes of power, the dotted lines indicate points of equal power.
AUDIENCE

	Man-made		*Natural*
Rectilinear	Urban	Curvilinear	Rural
Interior	Safe	Exterior	Dangerous
Private	Static	Public	Dynamic
Exclusive		Inclusive	

Midway between the extremes stand certain mediating spaces, such as gardens, parks, market squares and theatres, which bring many 'natural' qualities into the man-made sphere. It is no accident that Mark Antony makes such progress with his funeral oration in the Forum, because there he knows he is in public space and can get away with statements and actions that in the private world of the Senate House would cost him his life, as they had Caesar's.

Perhaps the commonest device is to counterpoint one type of space with another, either by contrasting natural and man-made spaces, as in the comedies of Shakespeare, or by examining contrasting types of man-made space. The history plays of Shakespeare oscillate between the high-status world of the court, set in the palace and the castle, and the low-status world of Eastcheap taverns. Brecht uses similar divisions between high- and low-status space, and, in *Arturo Ui*, for example, Ui's power is measured by the extent to which he takes the rules of his private space into public spaces such as the courts and City Hall. Some playwrights, among them John Arden and Ben Jonson, have shown special interest in making theatrical space turn back into real space, as in Arden's envisaged market setting for *The Workhouse Donkey*, or the market from which it derives in *Bartholomew Fair*.

In strict contrast to the rapidly shifting settings of much English-language theatre, the classical Greek and neo-classical French theatres have either in practice, or by force of aesthetic legislation, tended to obey what is called the *unity* of place. The theory is that, by setting a dramatic action in one place only, the illusion of verisimilitude so important to the play's emotional impact will not be disturbed. Thus all that we see of the action of, for example, Racine's masterly *Bérénice*, takes place in the waiting-area between two rooms, from which the protagonists emerge. The intensity of focus is extreme, and in this work there is no sense in which by obeying the unity of place Racine has surrendered any essential advantage of multiple set. Quite the opposite: the concentration of the play depends on the unity of place, which abets the intervention of the audience's imagination in the drama by its very asceticism. By contrast, the necessity of having to obey the unity of place at all costs is absurdly restrictive, especially since in a literal sense the unity of place is nearly always observed in performance, by virtue of its all taking place on the same designated space.

Particular attention is given in theatre to spaces which embody a balance, or synthesis, of the two types of spatial system – the garden, mythically the place of paradise, paramount among them. The garden is the *locus amoenus*, the pleasant place: it may, as in medieval and Renaissance culture, be protected by walls, a *hortus inclusus*, and it may well combine art and nature, pleasure and use, by growing fruits and vegetables while serving as a place of sport and recreation. It is the meeting-point of the art of man and the artlessness of nature. John of Gaunt, addressing Richard II, talks of England as a garden, a second Eden. In *Hamlet* Denmark is seen as a garden full of weeds, and the murder of King Hamlet is given an added tweak of savagery by being set in an orchard. As with the Fall of Eve, evil in a garden is doubly villainous.

The garden, with its designated boundaries, its spatial codes and art, is to that inchoate and vast space of the heath what the theatre is to the world; hence a further level of interest in it to the playwright. But natural outdoor space is not merely threatening and destructive. In *Cymbeline* the forces of renewal, Guiderius and Arviragus, come from the heath. Tom, alias Edgar, takes refuge on the heath, where the democracy of dispossession rules. Perdita is rediscovered in a rustic environment. Miranda is brought up on an island. But the characters, such as Jaques, who want to go on living in an environment where man seems ultimately unaccommodated are rare. Life in such spaces is hard, a battle with one's own will as well as with natural elements. Significantly, it is during battles that men make their one predatory claim on natural space, using it to line up their symmetric ranks of soldiers, who fight and die out of view from the city, far away from any garden.

It is perhaps because theatre itself has moved indoors that there has been a historical shift in the setting of plays from outdoors to indoors: much modern theatre is set firmly in the domestic world, in the kitchen or the living-room, as in the plays of Arnold Wesker or David Storey. Some of Brecht's most significant innovations in theatre consisted in showing the potential for epic theatre within the mundane setting. And in a tragedy such as Wedekind's *Spring Awakening*, or Chekhov's *The Seagull*, domestic constriction is shown to be one of the main causes of what happens. John Arden put the whole of a house on view in *Live Like Pigs*, exploiting the sociological information carried by the interior design of the 1950s council house to underpin the conflicts enacted in the house.

By contrast, Beckett in *Waiting for Godot* went back to the

Shakespearian empty stage, using the shock value of such a stage in a theatre still dominated by realism in set construction to enhance the feeling of alienation and strangeness. In a different way, Brecht also plays with the magic of emptiness – as, for example, in *The Caucasian Chalk Circle* when Grusha crosses the imagined ice bridge. Behind these uses of theatrical space, to highlight a real or imagined place or thing, is the Russian formalist principle of *defamiliarisation*, which argues that to see something in the real world properly one has to take it out of its familiar environment and place it in one in which it is defamiliarised, such as the theatre. Nothing is more defamiliarising than seeing isolated bits of real environments – such as chairs, or fruit or trees – on empty stages lit with white light.

Unity of place and the world stage

The theory of the unity of place, and the complementary unities of time and action, is traced, erroneously, back to Aristotle, and is particularly associated with 'classical' as opposed to 'Anglo-Saxon' theatre. But Shakespeare constantly exploits the literal unity of place in all performance – as, for example, in the second act of *Macbeth*: with one exception, all the scenes in this act take place in one continuous sequence in the castle courtyard, a fact that most editors ignore when they print the act as four rather than two scenes. First Banquo and Fleance enter, bearing a torch. Their manner suggests that, far from feeling secure in the yard, they are deeply apprehensive. Then Macbeth arrives, also bearing a torch: he converses with them. Banquo and Fleance leave, and with their going the courtyard turns from a shared, public part of the castle into a private place of soliloquy. Macbeth leaves to murder Duncan. The stage is empty. Lady Macbeth enters and takes his position, the substitution neatly suggesting a continuity of consciousness between the two. Macbeth returns, and the yard becomes their shared private space, a sign of their intimacy.

But not for long: a knocking, which seems at first to them like the pounding of their hearts, reminds us and them that they are in a courtyard, with an external door, and many internal ones. They leave, and the Porter enters, the official doyen of the space. He tells us this place is hell mouth, something we have begun to realise for ourselves. The knocking is then given human form, for Macduff demands admittance. He enters, reminding us of the architectural function of the courtyard as a place of arrival and departure, and then goes off into the castle to find the King. He re-enters with the news of Duncan's death, which confirms the Porter's belief that the yard is a place of spiritual as well as physical departure. With the alarm raised, the private courtyard becomes once more the central public space of the building. The overall effect of this sequence is to confirm in us the relativity of space – spatial codes reflect user attitudes and not just physical or architectural rules and conventions – and to remind us of the affinity between the performance yard of the Globe and the yard in Macbeth's castle.

Yet neither Macbeth's nor Shakespeare's 'yard' ever stops being a yard: indeed, the yard is ideally suited to be the place of public and private revelation because it is the spatial nexus of the castle, the centre of its goings-out and comings-in. A strong affinity exists, therefore, between the place of revelation in *Macbeth* and the place of disclosure in *Bérénice*. Such yards are *liminal* space (in Latin, *limen* means threshold) which connects inside and outside, the worlds of the public and the private domains. A garden is similarly liminal, in that it connects the world of the city and the house with that of the heath and the hovel.

In *Romeo and Juliet*, the most celebrated liminal space is the balcony, half in the house, half in the air, and it is crucial to our understanding of the lovers' relationship that they should reach each other over a balcony, rather than through the traditional marital entry, the front door. Büchner constantly has protagonists looking out of, or in through, windows, or sitting in the threshold of doors. In the climactic scene of *Spring Awakening*, Wedekind explores the liminal aspects of a graveyard, the junction point of life and death, and has a character appear masked, in an embodiment of the principle of liminality. Self-evidently, liminality is an aspect of relativity, particularly significant because it concerns itself with the point at, and means by, which something becomes something else.

Another way of reinforcing the potential liminality of all space is abruptly to change designated location, while still, literally, being in the same place. The last brief scene of Act II of *Macbeth* has us suddenly outside the castle, to hear of a storm so violent that by all the rules of nature and of naturalism we should have heard it in the castle courtyard – but we did not. Later, in Act IV, Shakespeare takes us for one scene to England. Büchner plays a similar trick when he takes Danton out of Paris for one brief scene in *Danton's Death*, to contemplate the city 'as it were through a lorgnette'. It is the only scene in the whole play when Danton leaves Paris, and yet it acts as a counterpoint to all the civic action.

Another effective approach to liminality is that taken by David Storey in *The Contractor*, in which a marquee is erected and then taken down on stage. The ostensible purpose of putting up the marquee is for a wedding-reception, but when we are not shown this reception we begin to realise that the play is more about enclosing space than about weddings. There is an affinity described between the act of set-building and the act of putting up a wedding-tent, and Storey builds a whole play upon an investigation of the process by which one space – here a garden – is transformed into a place of festival, and then returned to being a garden again. When the audience leaves the theatre it can no longer be sure whether to describe the garden as a garden, or as a garden without tent.

I have described the performance yard as a place of disclosure, a place in which truths are told and secrets revealed. For the most part theatrical space is a place of disclosure, but it is also a place of *closure*, in which endings are not merely recounted but shown. In Act II of *Macbeth*, Shakespeare keeps death within the realm of disclosure. We hear of Duncan's murder; we do not see it. This is done so as not to weaken the subsequent death of Lady Macduff and her children, which does bring death onto the stage, for this is the moment of closure on their lives which sets in train the closure of Macbeth's murderous career. In classical theory all such action, all closure, is to be kept off-stage. But even in classical practice, as at the end of *Oedipus Colonnus*, the mythic cycle closes on stage, though, here ironically, in the context of a secret disclosure by Oedipus to Theseus.

Lighting and light

As between set and setting, we may distinguish between the practical problem of *lighting* a production and the more complex issue of *light*. The relationship between light and performance has both an imaginative and a practical aspect: light is a dominant source of theatrical imagery, and one of the principal indicators of time.

The primary function of stage-lighting is to light the performers, to illuminate the performance space. At this level there is no essential difference between lighting and light. The secondary function of lighting is to act in a commentatorial or even interventionary manner in the action, to become an actant. There is no absolute need for this secondary function, and until the discovery of electricity there was little exploitation of it. But the power of electric lighting to express mood, and to organise our visual responses to environments and shapes, is so great that it has become perhaps the most significant element in the technical business of the theatre.

Illumination and technology

Before the development of modern stage-lighting techniques, the commonest solution to lighting a performance was to perform outdoors. But this posed a difficulty for the dramatist: how to establish temporal conventions within the plot and in particular to distinguish between night and day. In *Macbeth*, for example, a great deal of the play takes place at night, although in real time it would have been played in the afternoon on the Globe stage. The devices used to overcome the potential absurdities of night scenes played in blazing sunshine were twofold. First, characters would frequently refer to the time of day, either by direct reference to time, or by invitations to meals, bed or recreation. Secondly, an indicator of time of day or night was introduced into the action – as, for example, when night is established in Act II of *Macbeth* by the use of torches, and day by Macduff's telling us that it has dawned. In *Twelfth Night* we know that it is very late when Malvolio appears in his nightgown to remonstrate with the drunken and carousing Toby, Aguecheek and Feste. The lovers in *A Midsummer Night's Dream* fall asleep to indicate night, and Puck tells us about the effect of moonlight and darkness on our perception of shape and distance. In all instances the imagination is asked to create a light appropriate to the time and season.

The neatest emblem of the interrelationship between lighting and light is Lady Macbeth's candle. It casts a light of its own, and in modern stagings and films the flickering candlelight is frequently used to create the mood of suspense and threat which leads up to her suicide. But it is Macbeth himself who explains the metaphoric burden of the candle:

> Out, out, brief candle!
> Life's but a walking shadow, a poor player
> That struts and frets his hour upon the stage,
> And then is heard no more.
>
> (*Macbeth*, v.v.23–6)

The candle is none other than Lady Macbeth's life, soon to flicker out, and that very flickering reminds Macbeth forcibly of the shadowy player, who steps briefly into the light of the stage before vanishing again into the dark.

The candle is also the beginning of lighting-technology. By judicious control of the placement and quantity of candles (candlepower), quite complex effects can be achieved, as was already known to the neo-classical French theatre. Candle wicks do however, have to be trimmed, and the act length of seventeenth-century French theatre was in large measure determined by the need, every twenty minutes or so, to trim wicks. The British theatre lagged rather behind, and not till the mid eighteenth century did Garrick, under the influence of French theatre, move away from a single huge chandelier set over the front of the stage to a more elaborate distribution of candles around the set. The logistical difficulties of wick-trimming were considerable and the prospect of fire a virtual certainty. But there was a commensurate gain, in that the performance of *Hamlet* or *Macbeth* Garrick's audience saw was peculiarly atmospheric, with its mass of flickering lights. The actors faced another type of hazard, wax dripping in streams from the candles above their heads – a fact which made many of them wary of moving too much into the light. It also engendered a performance habit of acting with an upturned face, to catch the candlelight, one which persists to this day in classical dance. Overall, however, the combined effects of elaborate staging and crude lighting meant that the performer did little more in the seventeenth- and eighteenth-century indoor performance than enter the stage, stand and deliver his part and leave again.

As lighting began to improve, so the performer could think of moving more. The first major step forward in this direction was into gas lighting, one of the prime exponents of which was Henry Irving, who in the mid nineteenth century perfected the art of controlling the bluish tones of the gas lamp. Melodrama as a genre seems in particular to have flourished under gas light, and in the popular mind figures such as Jack the Ripper always stalk under foggy gas-lamps down dark inner-city alleys. One of the advantages gas lighting offered performers was greater security of movement, and elaborate fight scenes, using the whole stage area, became an increasingly popular part of indoor stagecraft, as they had been on the outdoor Elizabethan and Jacobean stage.

Gas was supplanted in the 1880s by electricity, now the dominant means of lighting the stage. There are two main kinds of stage light, the *flood* and the *spot*. While the flood has the task of general illumination, and typically uses a *fresnel* lens to diffuse the light, the spot directs light to a particular area and is generally used for special effect. The spot can be focused with a hard or soft edge, and with the help of an iris diaphragm can be reduced to a pinpoint – giving rise to the technical term *pinspot* for the single light that picks out just the performer's head. Such an effect was used to great effect by Richard Pilbrow in his lighting of *Camelot* at Drury Lane, when after a sumptuously colourful show Arthur's valedictory monologue was given under a white pinspot. Lamps are coloured up with the use of filters or *gels* placed in front of them, and as plastics technology has improved so has colour quality and fidelity.

The direction of the light and the area covered can be controlled either by *barn doors*, consisting of four metal flaps which can be angled to control the flood lamp, or by shutters in the profile. By using *gobos*, specially cut metal inserts in front of lamps, effects such as the dispersal of light through leaves can be achieved. Other effects frequently used are ultra-violet light, which makes things painted with special paint, or washed in modern detergents, glow; stroboscopic light, which flashes at disconcerting intervals; and laser light, which promised to revolutionise stage-lighting with its intensity and accuracy, but in fact is seldom used. If it becomes cheaper, the hologram, which enables the lighting-designer to create the illusion of a three-dimensional image using only light, may well gain ground in the theatre.

The cue as choric effect

Perhaps the most obvious advantage of modern lighting-systems, however, is the ease and speed with which changes can be made. As electrical control systems developed, it became possible to control the settings of an entire lighting-rig from a central lighting-box, on a single console. There no longer needed to be breaks for adjusting candles or a myriad of gas-lamps, which meant that the number and variety of lighting-changes could be radically increased. Advances in electronics have continued to revolutionise control systems for lights, both in the way the actual dimming-process itself works, and in the management of *cues*. A cue is simply a timing-convention in theatre: at a particular point a move, or a word, will act as cue for a change in lights, or sound, or both. With the help of computers, complex and lengthy cues can all be executed with perfect precision and timing. For example, lighting can exactly imitate the progress of light through a day, including the movement of the sun and shadows, by using the computer to effect a cue with infinite gradation. These advances have another valuable side effect: lighting-controls are now very light. Touring theatre can take professional lighting to venues with no facilities at relatively low cost and effort.

In some respects the lighting-cue has become the modern equivalent of the classical chorus. When in pantomime there is a bang and the lights suddenly drop, we know the villain is not far off. In a whodunnit the lights always go off just before the crime. By contrast, the slow emergence of pure, clean blue light at the end of Wagner's *Ring* signals that the Rhine has cleansed the corruption of the old gods and begun a new age. This particular cue depends partly on *speed*, partly on *intensity*, partly on *colour*, the three main elements of the cue.

Speed

One of the most powerful means of signalling dramatic tempo, especially sudden plot developments, is rapid changes of lighting-states. At the start of the *Agamemnon* by Aeschylus, a burning light in the east alerts the Watchman first to special attention and then to joy, because it is the long-awaited beacon of peace. Buzz Goodbody's decision suddenly to turn the lights off when Gloucester is blinded in *King Lear* made a dramatic connection between the blinding and our sudden inability to see the stage. At the end of *Ghosts*, by contrast, the blinding light required at the close begins as a dim off-stage fire, and then slowly grows to the blinding intensity of sunlight shining directly in our eyes, an effect impossible before the introduction of electric lighting into theatres. Abrupt changes of pace in lighting tend to disrupt the continuity of stage action, and are often used for this purpose. Cues that merely open and close scenes, as in light comedies, tend to make the lighting unobtrusive, the mere illumination of the performance space.

Intensity

There is a natural relationship between intensity and speed, as suggested in the long cues at the end of *The Ring* and *Ghosts*, but this relationship is predicated on naturalistic assumptions about the function of lighting. Brecht, by contrast, argued for performance in a single, intensely white lighting-state, partly in order to reinforce in the audience an awareness of the distinction between theatre and reality, partly to resist the temptation to cover over deficiencies in performance with clever stage-lighting. He claimed that too much variation in the intensity of light in the interests of naturalistic authenticity would obscure the essential message of the performance. Thus pure white light is intrinsic to his *alienation effect*.

Even in Brecht's white light, however, contrast and shadow are unavoidable properties of stage-lighting. Contrast and shadow divide the stage area into variable sections without the help of a set. So, by having two pools of light separated by darkness, two places can be created on a single performing-area.

Variations in intensity can be achieved in different ways. In a production of *The Winter's Tale*, directed by Trevor Nunn, the jealousy of Leontes was signified by the use of venetian blinds (jalousies) to disperse light shone onto the set from behind them. In David Storey's *The Contractor* the tent canvas has the effect of dispersing the light on stage into an even wash, which has a psychologically relaxing effect. Leaf effects are frequently employed for country and forest scenes. Intensity will also be one of the surest guides we are given to what time of day or night it is, and whether we are indoors or out. Productions which make use of simultaneous staging may well contrast two environments by lighting them in significantly different ways.

Variety can be achieved by occasional uses of sources of light other than electrical, such as candles, torches and flares. Bill Bryden's production of the *Mysteries* used a miner's lamp to convey a modern equivalent of the Harrowing of Hell by Jesus, the light of the world. The fire regulations, understandably if regrettably, make

the use of the most potent and atmospheric source of light, fire
itself, very infrequent in performance.

Colour

The iconographic significance of colour is not a theatrical discovery,
but it is used the whole time by the theatre. Wagner's *Ring* ends in
pure blue, the colour traditionally associated with the Virgin Mary.
Black denotes mourning, pinks and golds the safe and cheerful
mood of pantomime. Greens are for the forest and nature. Where
iconography can be very useful is when the mood and the colour are
clashed: in the discomfiture of Malvolio, the yellow stockings
against the black of his steward's dress are one of the main visual
sources of the joke. In *Macbeth* the movement of the green wood
against Macbeth's blackness signals the final retribution of nature.

Illumination and image

Light, in itself and in its daily and seasonal variations, is one of the
most potent sources of theatrical imagery, a point of direct
connection between the mind and the concrete world, as in the case
of Lady Macbeth's candle. The dominant image, hardly
surprisingly, is the sun, not least because of a fortuitous but
powerful pun in English on the word (son/sun). It is the blinding
light, the source of heat and power, the emblem of absolute
authority, the lack of which is impotence, death and grief. The
beginning of *Richard III* establishes a cruelly deceptive sunny
mood:

> Now is the winter of our discontent
> Made glorious summer by this sun of York,
> And all the clouds that lour'd upon our house
> In the deep bosom of the ocean buried.
> (I.i.1–4)

The light of summer is equated with peace, and later with dalliance.
It is contrasted with darkness and rain, the signs of winter. The
irony is soon transparent, that this summer is to be of brief duration.
The sun may also look like a threatening red eye, an image derived
from Egyptian, and later Christian, belief in the sun as the eye of the

world, which is how it is commonly depicted in Baroque iconography.

In *Samson Agonistes*, the sun and moon are turned by Samson into emblems of his own condition, the darkness being like an eclipse:

> O dark, dark, dark, amid the blaze of noon,
> Irrecoverably dark, total Eclipse
> Without all hope of day.
> O first created Beam, and thou great Word,
> Let there be light, and light was over all,
> Why am I thus bereaved thy prime decree?
> The Sun to me is dark
> And silent as the Moon,
> When she deserts the Night,
> Hid in her vacant interlunar cave.
>
> (lines 80–9)[5]

By personalising light so intensely, Samson makes us acutely aware as audience that we can see him but he cannot see us. In this he seems like the naturalistic actor, seen by the audience but never allowed to admit that he sees them. At the same time, Samson equates light with understanding, an equation summarised in the ambiguity of *illumination* or *enlightenment* as both physical and intellectual understanding.

Props

The inanimate agents in stage actions or transactions are known as props. Murders have to be committed with knives or guns, messages have to be exchanged by letter, love has to be sealed by tokens. So the commonest props are letters, daggers, rings, purses and items of food. Props may be distinguished from elements of the set by being easily portable, and when they change hands, either by design or accident, it is to advance the plot or enable its advancement. They also tend, as with weapons, crowns, musical instruments or tools, to establish what status or occupation a person has, and with it a value system.

Props may be used for special effect, to the extent that they become temporary actants. In Dario Fo's *Can't Pay, Won't Pay,* there is an exploding cuckoo clock, which plays such a role in the climax that it might be better understood as an actant rather than a prop, if prop it is, for it remains anchored to the set throughout. In J. B. Priestley's *An Inspector Calls*, the telephone is so forceful a presence that it becomes more an actant than a prop, or natural part of the drawing-room set. In Menotti's opera *The Telephone*, this is indeed what the telephone becomes. In endlessly tedious detective series, telephones are props in every sense. In more recent years, directors such as Grotowski have experimented with actors themselves performing the role of props and set, which renders the attempt at definition almost meaningless.

Some props, such as Lady Macbeth's candle, are simultaneously part of the lighting. Others are part of the costume, in the way that the murderer's dagger is an intrinsic part of his identity, as is the King's crown. In *Troilus and Cressida* the scarf, an item of clothing, becomes a central prop and symbol first of Cressida's love for, then of her betrayal of, Troilus. The most powerful use of this device is in *Othello*, during which the accidental loss of a special handkerchief becomes the agent of Othello's madness and Desdemona's death. To Othello, the handkerchief is a devilish character, an actor in the play of his wife's infidelity. In the medieval *Second Shepherds' Play*, Mac the sheep-stealer has secreted his stolen lamb in a manger; his fellow shepherds come looking for him and the lamb, but Mac manages to convince them that the lamb is a baby. So the off-stage audience, who have been asked to believe that a sheepskin or bundle of cloth is a lamb, now see how the on-stage audience are made to see the bundle as a baby. Thus a prop becomes a character.

Puck characterises himself as half-way between protean actor and protean prop:

> I jest to Oberon and make him smile
> When I a fat and bean-fed horse beguile,
> Neighing in likeness of a filly foal;
> And sometime lurk I in a gossip's bowl
> In very likeness of a roasted crab
> And when she drinks against her lips I bob,
> And on her withered dewlap pour the ale.
> The wisest aunt, telling the saddest tale,
> Sometime for three-foot stool mistaketh me;
> Then slip I from her bum, down topples she,

> And 'tailor' cries, and falls into a cough;
> And then the whole quire hold their hips and laugh . . . .
> *(Midsummer Night's Dream*, ii.i.44–55)

Puck is fairy/human, an animal, a fruit and a stool, and he makes fun of the world by imitating props, playing with perceptions. In due course he will make himself find out what it is like to be on the receiving end of trickery, for the love juice misfires on him.

Through his agency, and through the agency of the ass's head prop, Bottom's identity is changed, the ass in him being given, for a while at least, the upper hand. In this act of transformation, we not only see the potential in Bottom for becoming any number of animals, or indeed combinations of several, but we also experience his being a protean prop in a play of perceptions, something he vaguely intuits when he wakes up from his dream to find that it has 'no bottom'.

Complex props often have their meaning explained in some detail as part of the action. This commonly occurs when a character reflects on the prop at the point when its existence or nature matters most to him. Richard II, for example, contemplates his crown, and as he does so, he reflects on it as an emblem of his state:

> for within the hollow crown
> That rounds the mortal temples of a king
> Keeps death his court; and there the antic sits,
> Scoffing his state, and grinning at his pomp;
> Allowing him a breath, a little scene,
> To monarchise, be fear'd and kill with looks;
> Infusing him with self and vain conceit,
> As if this flesh which walls about our life
> Were brass impregnable; and humour'd thus,
> Comes at the last and with a little pin
> Bores through his castle wall and farewell king.
> *(Richard II*, iii.ii.160–70)

The endless, hollow circle of the crown becomes its own condemnation of the wearer, a weak and foolish king. And this crown, by association with the wooden O which it probably in reality is, takes Richard's thoughts to acting, and to the all-pervading metaphor of the world stage. Simplest and most poignant of all the meanings, however, is that Richard, by his own shortcomings, has turned what should be as natural a part of him as the crown of his head into a mere prop in a tawdry historical melodrama in which he has the leading role.

Costume and make-up

Costume and make-up constitute the bridge between the animate and the inanimate in performance; on the peg and in the box they are mere materials; on the performer they become an essential part of his self. They affect the way a character moves and the expressions he makes and are directly influential on his behaviour. They are also decorative in function, contributing to the overall look of the performance and giving figurative clues to its meaning.

The practical purposes of costume and make-up are in themselves manifold: they establish age, sex, rank, taste, identity, special features, nationality, religion, social affiliation, and become an index of character and personality. If both are strictly located in period, they will also bear a particular historical and sociological value system within them. The more uniform a costume is, the less specificity of personal information it offers, and there tends to be a direct relationship between complexity of costume and significance of character. In a wider sense, both costume and make-up complement set and lighting in the way they offer concepts of shape, colour, time and style to the audience. Thus they have partly the function of being a mobile aspect of the setting.

For the performer, getting into costume and making up is, whatever the period of the setting, one of the liminal moments in the establishment of his role. The assumption of the clothes of another self is integral to the assumption of the psychology of that self. Yet, as Shakespeare has Feste remind us, 'cucullus non facit monachum' – clothes do not make the man – and often dramatic effect is derived from false expectations raised by costume, either through disguise or through special circumstances.

Stereotypes

Our response to costume is in part a response to indexical stereotypes: kings wear crowns, beggars have staffs and begging-bowls, soldiers and sailors wear uniform. Because these stereotypes and their associated expectations about identity and nature are so strong, their subversion is commensurately powerful. When we see a king wearing no clothes, especially when he thinks he is dressed, we find it funny – funnier than if we see a commoner wearing none, which we probably find odd or indecent. When we see a king, maddened by grief and folly, tearing his clothes off in a storm, we experience a mixture of amazement, anger, grotesque laughter and grief which makes that scene, in *King Lear*, uniquely painful in the theatre. In that same scene, we see a noble man, Edgar, wearing no clothes at all, and a fool wearing a ragged motley, his uniform. Madness and dispossession, which reach their climax in the storm, are reinforced by the deliberate subversion of our expectations of how such characters as kings, nobles and clowns should be clothed.

In *Henry V*, we see another aspect of the subversion of the relationship between clothes and identity, when the King, worn down with the care of office, dons a disguise as he had done as prince, to go round his people by night. The move turns out to be a double-edged one, because his troops feel none too comfortable when they discover they have been spied on by a man who is a king but does not declare himself by his clothes and manner to be one. Shakespeare was so intrigued by this problem that *Measure for Measure* is made to turn on the behaviour of just such a leader in disguise.

A response of a different kind is caused by the expectations certain colours and styles of dress and overall appearance raise about mood. Black betokens mourning, and in *Twelfth Night* Olivia is in black, with a veil. Malvolio is in black, as befits a member of a household in mourning, but is persuaded to wear yellow stockings for love. The lover Benedick in *Much Ado about Nothing* offers a classic picture of clothing in disarray, a comic Lear:

> here is no appearance of fancy in him, unless it be fancy that he hath to strange disguises; as to be a Dutchman today, a Frenchman to-morrow; or in the shape of two countries at once, as a German from the waist downward, all slops, and a Spaniard from the hip upward, no doublet. (III.ii.28–34)

In addition he is unshaven, of a yellowy complexion and complains of toothache. Hamlet is in similar disarray:

My lord, as I was sewing in my closet,
Lord Hamlet, with his doublet all unbrac'd,
No hat upon his head, his stockings fouled,
Ungart'red and down-gyved to his ankle;
Pale as his shirt . . . he comes before me.
                                    (*Hamlet*, ii.i.77–84)

What is unclear in this scene is whether his disarray is caused by
love, fear, madness, or a combination of all three. Whichever the
cause, psychological upheaval commonly has some effect on dress,
which underlines the fact that it is not merely what one wears in
performance that gives the audience information, but how one
wears it. As with lighting, it is often through changes in dress or
appearance that changes in the underlying action are made visible.

Molière uses class conventions of dress in *Dom Juan* to enable
Don Juan to escape from a difficult situation. Don Juan forces
Sganarelle to change clothes with him, leaving the nobly dressed
Sganarelle to deal with the ensuing problem. In this classic instance,
our expectations of identity are shown to be so strongly determined
by dress that we become incapable of recognising an individual's
face. The relationship between class and dress is so close that, in
Dekker's play *Fortunatus*, it nearly costs Fortunatus his life: he
makes the mistake of spending a lot of money while still poorly
dressed; it is then assumed that he must have stolen the money, and
he is lucky to escape with his life. In Shakespeare's comedies, girls
disguise themselves as boys to travel more safely, or to get
employment. In *Sleuth*, disguise forms the basis of the entire second
half of the play, Shaffer using expectations of uniform to prevent
the audience from seeing the theatrical trick. In this context,
'make-up' seems nicely ambiguous as a term, the 'made-up' face
being appropriately identified as fictional, an assumption of a false
expression.

Masks

A mediating-point between costume and make-up is the mask,
whether as a blank and expressionless screen covering the face or as
a figurative representation of a particular human or animal original.
It is thought that the classical Greek actor was masked (though
exactly how is open to dispute), the mask emphasising the

representative nature of the role portrayed. Brecht used blank masks both as a staging and as an alienation device. Yet, as the verse plays of W. B. Yeats demonstrate, the wearing of a mask may have the opposite effect on the audience to distancing: in its very blankness the mask implicitly invites the audience to project onto it the imagined expressions of the face in the same way that Shakespeare asks audiences to project an imagined setting onto an empty stage.

In the traditional *commedia dell'arte* theatre, masks were used to depict stereotypic characters, using a dominant expression, sign of age or temperament as an index of role. Masks in such circumstances were a theatrical short-hand, saving the need for establishment of individual identity by referring to physical or psychological type. Brecht's use of mask was predicated on the principle of typicality, though for political rather than aesthetic reasons. In Marxist aesthetics and politics, the individual is held to have no place, the class being all important. By masking an actor, Brecht turned an individual into a type.

In the closing scene of *Leonce and Lena*, Büchner encapsulates the essence of the theatrical mask. Valerio, the fool, has brought his master and mistress, Leonce and Lena, back to the kingdom of Popo to be married. He takes off a potentially infinite series of masks from his own face and then introduces Leonce and Lena as life-sized puppets:

PETER.   Who are you?
VALERIO.   How should I know? (*He slowly takes off a succession of masks.*) Am I this? or this? or this? In fact, I'm getting quite frightened, I could just sort of peel myself, defoliate myself away. . . . But my real purpose in coming was to announce to this high and honoured gathering that this very moment the two world famous automatons have arrived, and that I myself am perhaps the third and most remarkable of the species, if only I had any idea who I really am, which should be no surprise to anyone since I have no idea whatsoever what I am talking about which makes it highly probable that someone is making me talk like this, and that it is in fact merely pumps, valves and windpipes saying everything. (*With rasping tone*) You will observe here Ladies and Gentlemen, two persons of opposite sexes, a male and a female, and a man and a woman.

Nothing but art and technology, cardboard paper and clockwork.   (III.iii)[6]

The scene has two effects: the first, created by the unmasking of Valerio, is to call in question the notion of self within the theatre, each self being in fact infinitely redolent of other possible selves. This is different from the purpose of the religious mask, which is to forge a link between man and the divine, by allowing the god to enter the man through the agency of the mask. In theatre the stripping of masks is in pursuit of no goal other than itself, for, as Valerio says, inside the last mask is nothing at all. In religious ritual, entering the mask is entering trance or ecstasy, leaving it is a return to consciousness. The second effect is to open up the question of the performer's nature, as free agent or as puppet. This issue was to gain in immediacy and significance as the nineteenth century progressed, and still today is at the basis of the debate between director's and performer's theatre.

The question of masks has profound implications for our understanding of performance as a whole. Many religious rituals involve dancers or celebrants donning masks and, in effect becoming the mask's persona. Yeats intended such an identification in performance, the dancer becoming the dance, the mask-wearer becoming the mask. In using a mask, therefore, an actor is tapping a tradition of ritualistic performance, implicit in which is the identification of the performer with what he performs. It is harder, therefore, to maintain the simultaneity of being and representation in a mask, the masked performer and his audience tending to identification with his role.

Costume drama

Costume and make-up can become ends in their own right in the pageant or costume drama, a form popular with amateurs on large community occasions, lord mayor's or county shows. As such they tap old traditions of royal and civic entry ceremonies, and ritual diplomatic display, such as guards of honour; they also have the function of giving visible form and substance to history. Special types of performance event, such as ballroom dancing, or sport, or military parades, also have a strong emphasis on costume, especially uniform costume, which distinguishes visually between participants and observers.

Problems can, however, occur when performers are dressed in costumes requiring them to behave in ways wholly unfamiliar to them, with the result that they are costumed as Tudor kings and queens but speak and move like late-twentieth-century bourgeois. This happens most commonly on television, where productions are sold on the authenticity of their reconstruction of period life rather than their dramatic value. The results arc deadly, not least to the productions themselves, for one wrong button – and hawk-eyed viewers ensure there is always one – rocks the aesthetic conception to its foundations.

Nudity

Nudity in performance is as much 'costume' as any clothes, but is hedged around with the taboos of sexuality and privacy. These taboos are not fixed, as attitudes to clothing-habits on beaches over the past decade show. But there is still a particular problem about nudity within performance, because the experience of nakedness is intensified. As a consequence, the promise of naked girls in sex scenes can be used gratuitously to draw public attention, as many shows did after the reform of censorship in Britain in 1968. It can likewise be misunderstood as gratuitous by an audience committed to attacking all theatrical nudity, come what may. Certain conventions have established themselves within the concept of nudity. Rear views are acceptable in a way that 'full frontals' are not. It is more acceptable for a woman to show her breasts than her pubic hair, and more acceptable for a woman to show pubic hair than a man – or, if not more acceptable, more frequently in demand, since it seems that men are far more interested in nudity than women are.

For the performer, the problem of nudity may be less one of overcoming his own feelings of reluctance to undress, or appear naked, in public than one of sustaining a representational sense both for himself and for the audience in performance. It is one thing to represent Julius Caesar in a toga, another to represent him with no clothes at all. The naked body admits of far less perceptual ambiguity than the clothed body, which is also one reason why

eroticism is more readily conveyed by scanty or suggestive clothing
than by none at all.

Look and role

Stage make-up is used for both practical and decorative purposes.
At a practical level, it is a vital aid in the creation of naturalistic
character-building, enabling performers to age, to rejuvenate, to
acquire or lose scars, deformities, teeth or hair. At a decorative
level, it may be used to adorn, as off-stage make-up is, or as part of
the whole look of a production. Certain genres, such as Westerns,
use different make-up conventions as an index of cultural
adherence. Indians make up, white men do not. White men 'black
up' to perform song-and-dance routines.

Make-up may either confirm assumptions we have about a role by
creating a face and an appearance compatible with our expectations
or it may challenge our assumptions by contradicting or stretching
them. Since we expect old people to be grey-haired and to have lines
on the faces and wrinkled skin, young performers playing older
roles may be put through elaborate make-up to establish an
authentic image of age. Likewise, older performers may put on
thickly textured make-up to recover an appearance of youth and
beauty. But we might play Richard III with a handsome face and
undeformed body to challenge the melodramatic association of
crooked physiognomy with evil nature. The beautiful devil is even
more to be feared than his hideous counterpart.

As with costume, too much attention can be paid to make-up, to
the point when it, not the performer, becomes the centre of attention
and effort. It is possible for a performer to play a character
substantially different in age from himself without the aid of
make-up, using the power of designation to invite the audience to
conceive of him as a different age from the one his face suggests.

Chapter 5

Their Brave State: Movement and Sound

While performance synthesises the dialectical opposites of movement and sound, these domains themselves are dialectical in nature. The performer's movement, choreographed or not, is given energy and shape by the immobile shape and confines of the stage

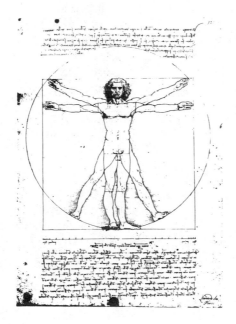

and set and by his own control of the relationship between movement and stasis.

The sounds he makes, pitched or unpitched, are pointed by the silences of those listening on- and off-stage, and by the underlying recognition that silence may be the final resolution of all sound as stasis may be of all movement. Silence and absence may be deliberately enigmatic. Where, for example, does Lear's Fool go? What all stage movement and sound have in common is *significance*. The scratching of a nose, the slightest stammer or hesitation on stage has, or is thought by an audience to have, significance, despite the fact that off-stage such details would be overlooked or unnoticed.

Within the categories of movement and sound there are various complementary dialectical forces, which are listed below. A given moment of performance can thus be analysed as a product of any number of these dialectical forces in a specific configuration:

Movement

Movement	Stasis
Free	Restricted
Dominant	Subordinate
Affective	Occupational
Natural	Mechanical
Individual	Ensemble
Improvised	Choreographed
Regular	Irregular
Conscious	Instinctive
Intended	Involuntary

Sound

Sound	Silence
Natural	Mechanical
Amplified	Non-amplified
Verbal	Non-verbal
Articulated	Noise
Rhythmic	Arhythmic
Individual	Ensemble
,Conscious	Instinctive

Intended	Involuntary
Pitched	Unpitched
Vocal	Instrumental
Articulated	Noise

Movement

Movement and stasis

Stage movement is the product of the mediation of ideas and feelings through actants. It is the visible expression of thought, the embodied action. Its physical aspects are determined by the principles of anatomy and physiology, its emotional roots are in behavioural patterns encoded in individuals and cultures. It supports speech, through gesture and facial expression, but equally it constitutes a language in its own right, as the sophisticated stage-movement dialects of dance and mime amply demonstrate. Movement signifies life, energy, consciousness.

The performer's principal concern with movement is as an index of character: how one moves largely defines how one is perceived. We may divide the concept of movement as a function of character into three main categories: (1) *expression* (facial movement), (2) *gesture* (head, trunk and hands), (3) *locomotion* (legs). These categories are in descending order of significance.

EXPRESSION

The most mobile, sophisticated and significant part of the performer's body is the face, especially the eyes and the mouth. The face gives conscious and unconscious signals about mood, attitude, state of health and attention. Its dominant signals are smiles and laughter to represent pleasure, welcome, amusement and interest, and frowns and tears for anger, grief, disapproval and concern. Performers seldom need to rehearse how to generate such expressions, though making them convincing constitutes one of the greatest demands placed on their skills.

Such signals are accepted literally at face value by an audience: when a character smiles he is happy and open, when he cries he is sad. But dramatists commonly subvert normal assumptions about the meanings of expression to create tension, doubt or comedy. Hamlet sees Claudio as a 'smiling villain', the smile luring him into a false sense of security. This is a classic emblem of the devilish schemer, who assumes a particular facial expression to deceive. When Richard III seduces Anne in *Richard III*, I.ii, the emotional structure of their confrontation is represented by the genuine expressions of anger, shame and confusion shown by Anne and the false faces of Richard, used to give visual credence to the falsity of his tongue. Behind the scene lies the common wisdom that 'false hearts' express themselves in 'false faces'.

The effect of the false face is to deceive the eyes, and thus the heart (the reactions) of another. The false face may be assumed for various reasons. Richard, like Arturo Ui, uses his control of his face, and its concomitant control of the emotions, for political and personal ends of a devious and evil kind. Viola, by contrast, controls her face to disguise her vulnerable female identity, though this in turn has unfortunate consequences – Olivia falls in love with her/him:

> Disguise, I see thou art a wickedness
> Wherein the pregnant enemy does much.
> How easy is it for the proper-false
> In women's waxen hearts to set their forms!
> Alas, our frailty is the cause, not we!
> For such as we are made of, such we be.
> (*Twelfth Night*, II.ii.25–30)

The moral is that honesty in expression is always desirable, if hard to achieve in practice.

Not surprisingly, eyes are the subject of constant theatrical concern – weeping, shining, searching, seeing. In classic iconography the eyes are 'windows to the heart', the light of day and of God shining through them into the soul. Shifty eyes are a sure sign of evil. Men are privileged to look at women, but if women look at men it suggests immodesty:

> MARGARET.   And how you may be converted I know not; but
>   methinks you look with your eyes as other women do.
> BEATRICE.   What pace is this that thy tongue keeps?
> (*Much Ado about Nothing*, III.iv.79–84)

In mumming-plays, the Doctor is commonly portrayed as one-eyed, indicating that he sees both with his eyes and with his mind, while the goddess Fortune is blind. Tiresias the blind seer has lost the power of outward sight, but knows the future.

The dominant function of the mouth is the generation and articulation of speech and other sounds. It and its constituent organs, the lips, teeth and tongue, are a rich source of expression, from biting and spitting to kissing. When Malvolio is duped, he is asked to smile, an expression he as a puritan never wears. 'I will smile; I will do everything that thou wilt have me', is his exit line in *Twelfth Night*, II.v. The result is entertainment for us, and ridicule for him. The most elaborate study of the disembodied mouth is Beckett's *Not I*, in which the mouth is represented as having an existence and power of action independent of all other organs. This gives substance to a common Renaissance preoccupation with the disjunction between words and meanings, the disembodied mouth speaking words behind which lie no moral values. Hamlet is worried by 'Words, mere words, no matter from the heart', and this aspect of his dilemma has a strongly contemporary flavour as linguistics and semiotics explore the seemingly arbitrary relationship between signs (words) and what they signify (meanings).

In *Romeo and Juliet*, Shakespeare clinches the relationship between verbal and visual forms of expression in the extended conceit of the face as book. Lady Capulet tries to persuade Juliet of Paris's virtues:

> Read o'er the volume of young Paris' face
> And find delight writ there with beauty's pen;
> Examine every married lineament
> And see how one another lends content;
> And what obscur'd in this fair volume lies
> Find written in the margent of his eyes.
> This precious book of love, this unbound lover
> To beautify him only lacks a cover.
>
> (I.iii.82–9)

Her synthesis of word and image is analogous to the process in chemistry whereby two atoms react together to form molecules. The molecules of theatrical expression are formed out of the reaction of words with images.

GESTURE

After the face, and frequently co-ordinated with it, the performer's most expressive instruments are the hands and fingers. Hands work. Hands are agents in actions – they hold other hands, daggers, swords, letters and cups; but they intervene directly, lending force to verbal expression and giving substance to physical encounters. Lady Macbeth becomes obsessed with cleaning her blood-stained hands. Pilate washes his hands in the Mystery cycles with great displays of self-excuse. Audiences, by contrast, use their hands to express appreciation and even, when clapping rhythms, to join in. Fingers point, summon, clasp. They also leave behind unmistakable prints, without which the world's detective stories would be considerably the poorer.

Most powerfully, hands and fingers are the first points of touch between two bodies, and thus the first signals of intimacy and trust. Leontes first puts out his hand to touch the statue of Hermione, and with his hand feels her unexpected warmth. In *Romeo and Juliet* touching, kissing and religious devotion are all interfused:

> ROMEO.   If I profane with my unworthiest hand
>   This holy shrine, the gentle fine is this:
>   My lips, two blushing pilgrims, ready stand
>   To smooth that rough touch with a tender kiss.
> JULIET.   Good pilgrim, you do wrong your hand too much,
>   Which mannerly devotion shows in this;
>   For saints have hands that pilgrims' hands do touch,
>   And palm to palm is holy palmers' kiss. (I.v.91–8)

At the close of *Romeo and Juliet*, the lovers die by their own hands – in Romeo's case, by co-ordinating hand, eye and lips to drink poison.

Fingers point to identify, as Demetrius and Chiron, who rape Lavinia in *Titus Andronicus*, well know – for they cut off her hands and pull out her tongue in self-protection. But fingers may also form the chink through which Pyramus and Thisbe whisper in *A Midsummer Night's Dream*, a compound of practical expediency and classic sexual suggestion. In Middleton's and Rowley's *The Changeling*, De Flores has to cut off Alsemero's finger with his ring to take it to Beatrice–Joanna as evidence. This disembodied digit turns into an index of accusation, pointed at the dissembling pair.

Hands and arms together engage in action. They fight, wrestle, shake and embrace. Most movingly, they carry the dead. When Imogen is thought dead in *Cymbeline*, Arviragus carries her in in his arms:

> BELARIUS.   Look, here he comes,
> And brings the dire occasion in his arms . . .   (IV.ii.196–7)

Even more tragically, Lear bears the dead Cordelia in his arms:

> LEAR.   Howl, howl, howl, howl! O, you are men of stones!
> Had I your tongues and eyes, I'd use them so
> That heaven's vault should crack. (*King Lear*, v.iii.256–8)

The image is doubly resonant in performance: Lear's mobility contrasts with Cordelia's immobility; his upright form carries her prone one in a cross-shaped emblem of grief. The image is so powerful because it embodies its own dialectic.

LOCOMOTION

There is nothing intrinsically remarkable about the fact that Lear enters. For performance to take place, performers have to make entries. What strikes us is that he, old and frail as he is, is carrying the heavy burden of the unexpectedly dead Cordelia. That Lear moves is unremarkable: that Cordelia does not move is remarkable. That Lear can carry her is astonishing.

The legs are naturally the least expressive part of the body, yet without them most performance would not be possible. From the simple question of the mechanics of entry and exit to the elaborate movements of ballet, mime or stage fighting, the legs constitute the essential precondition of the performance process. Beckett fully perceives the extent of the relationship between theatre and movement, for the end of *Waiting for Godot* is an instruction to Vladimir and Estragon not to move. Immobility ends action and consciousness: the play stops. In *Play*, Beckett goes further and has his actors immobilised up to the neck, with the result that the audience is confronted throughout with the absence of locomotion. In a slightly less drastic, but perhaps more dramatic, vein, Büchner has all three of his central protagonists, Danton, Woyzeck and Leonce, sit or lie on the ground at the moments of their greatest stress. They refuse locomotion as the most emphatic statement of their misery and powerlessness that they can make.

In *Richard II*, Shakespeare builds one of his finest speeches around the same motif:

> RICHARD.   For God's sake let us sit upon the ground
> And tell sad stories of the death of kings.   (III.ii.155–6)

The fact that the King should sit upon the ground is the simplest, yet most effective, indication of his fall.

A modern aspect to man's relationship with the ground, with womb–tomb earth, is explored in Arnold Wesker's *Roots*. Wesker presents the deracination of the rural labouring classes in their drift to the towns and cities during the Industrial Revolution as the source of their disenfranchisement. Lack of power is symbolised by rootless feet. Contact not just with the ground but with one's own ground is the centre of the psychology and politics of independence and freedom. This has important implications for the performer's relationship with his own plot of ground, the stage. His power of action and expression will stem from his ability to make himself at home and at ease on it.

While Beckett denies his performers mobility as part of a wider investigation of the performance process, immobility may be used in other ways in the definition of character or plot. In *Whose Life Is It Anyway?* the central protagonist is immobilised by his illness, and this very immobility gives his wish to die force. Kings or emperors, by contrast, may choose to be carried, giving their political and personal dominance expression in the physical subordination of others. Antony's death in *Antony and Cleopatra* is made all the more agonising by the fact that we see him, the noblest soldier, being hauled ignominiously up into the monument, too weak to move.

The issue of locomotion is by no means confined to human actants. The use of elaborate stage machinery to make sets move confers on the inanimate performance environment some of the properties of the performer, even if the set differs from the performer in being moved as opposed to possessing the independent power of locomotion. Shakespeare, however, challenges even this distinction, at least perceptually, when he has the wood of Birnam move to Dunsinane, and a wall move on- and off-stage, as well as speak. In both cases, parts of the organic as well as the inorganic environment that we do not expect to move are suddenly able to do so, in a startling demonstration of the relativity of states of matter.

In his theory of movement, Laban locates the centre of movement in the centre of the body. I do not wish to suggest that he is wrong, but would suggest that he is telling only half the story. Movement proceeds as much from the ground as from the centre of the body, and there is a dialectical tension between the two conceptual and practical centres of expression – the feet and the solar plexus – which is essential to the integration of physiology and aesthetics on which stage movement of all kinds relies.

The integration of aesthetics and physiology is at the heart of the Pygmalion myth, perhaps the *Ur*-myth of performing. The spirit of role enters the individual performer's body, and for a time they interact to create dramatic expression. But at the close of the play they part, the performer's body from the theatre, the role from the body. At Cleopatra's death, her body sinks towards its progenitor the ground, while her spirit soars to the sky. At the last, the dialectic resolves itself not in synthesis but in fission.

Free and restricted

Just as action in performance tends to spring from conflict, and from evil, so it is restricted rather than free movement that generates suspense and emotion. Throughout *A Doll's House*, Nora is compared to a bird, despite the fact that she is in a social and marital cage. This image of restriction is all the stronger when at the close she flies out of the cage, slamming the door behind her. Lear, by contrast, when in *King Lear*, v, he is dispatched to prison, comforts himself with the thought that he and Cordelia will 'sing like birds i'the'cage'. Restriction of movement is the most obvious sign of the power one person may have over another; it is also the state's most effective means of punishing its critics or fallen leaders.

In *Samson Agonistes*, the blind and powerless Samson is both physically and emotionally chained:

> A little onward lend thy guiding hand
> To these dark steps, a little further on;
> For yonder bank hath choice of Sun or shade.

There am I wont to sit, when any chance
Relieves me from my task of servile toil . . . .
(lines 1–5)

The combination of the word 'sit' with the image of a great hero put
to servile work creates an intense feeling of constriction which only
Samson's final liberating movement of pulling down the temple
over his head will alleviate.

The question of immobility had its grotesque and parodic
manifestation in Falstaff, the man who was so fat he could hardly
move. This aspect of him is encapsulated in the scene in *Henry IV,
Part 1* in which Falstaff is thought by Hal to have died in battle:

What, old acquaintance! Could not all this flesh
Keep in a little life? . . . (*Exit.*)

FALSTAFF (*rising up*).   . . . The better part of valour is
discretion; in the which better part I have saved my
life.   (v.iv.102–20)

Hal's agility, and fitness to rule, are set off by the mountain of dead
flab that so cynically comes back to life. For all this, Hal's Roman
counterpart, Julius Caesar, would rather have about him men who
are fat. Lean men are rivals for power.

Dominant and subordinate

The relationship between freedom and restriction in movement has
another aspect, in that freedom to move easily in space is an index of
status. Behaviour may be substantially determined by status, a
measure of the relative importance of a character within the
sociology of the action. Status may be a reflection of class
adherence; it may reflect position within a class. In the world of
Eastcheap, Falstaff has the highest status: he is its king. In the
wider world of contemporary politics he has less status, and, when
eventually rejected by Hal, none at all. Hal's own position as heir is
complex, for, while he is born into high status, that status has only
formal significance so long as his father lives. He reflects the
uncertainty this generates in him by oscillating uneasily between the
court of Westminster and Falstaff's court in Eastcheap.

Status is a measure of relative *dominance* and *subordination* of characters within an action. Dominance may be achieved through rank, force, intellect and wit, or through love, each form having its own code of movement. The dominant person in the relationship defines how the subordinate moves, and the subordinate adapts his body language to respond to the signals given out by the dominator. Dominance may be established in a play from the outset – as, for example, by the formal entry of a king. In *King Lear*, we see all the dominance of Lear in the way he enters for the opening scene. It is the subject's duty to bow to the king, the master to the servant, the maid to her mistress. But, where dominance is so apparent at the start of an action, one can feel confident that it will be challenged in the course of the play. Tension or rebellion is signalled by a degree of reluctance in the subject to accept continuing subordination. For example, Bolingbroke's departure for exile in *Richard II* may well be accompanied by a less than dutiful bow of allegiance to his sovereign. Dominance in highly structured societies tends to be *linear* – that is, there is a chain of power in which everyone knows his place. Tension arises from attempts to break or reforge the chain, as witnessed by intrigue, rebellion or subversion.

The moves of subordination are familiar enough: bows, curtseys, walking backwards out of someone's presence, deferential postures, running away or lying prone. These are complemented by their opposites to signal dominance, reinforced by a direct and steady gaze. A favourite device in comedy is to subvert status by undignified movement: a bishop slipping on a banana skin or losing his gaiters is, because of his status, funnier than the same happening to a young boy. In tragedy, a fall from dignity and status becomes the visible sign of lost power. Lear with no entourage and Othello writhing in epilepsy are agonising evidence of their enemies' success. When dominance is at issue, there are fights; when issues are resolved there are royal entries, or dances, or weddings – large, formally structured patterns of movement reflecting the crossing of a threshold from one era to another in personal or national history. At such thresholds, ritualised movement becomes the main agent of myth.

Dominance and subordination may, however, be of a different and psychologically more complex nature, as is commonly the case in intimate relationships in which both behavioural traits may be discerned simultaneously in the same person. The noble warrior invincible in the field is subordinate to a woman, as Samson to

Delilah or David to Bathsheba. Love, hate or kinship-bonding may
create triangular patterns of dominance: *A* may dominate *B*, *B*
dominate *C* and *C A*, so generating a more intense form of power
struggle than linear clashing. In the classic Arthurian triangle,
Arthur dominates Launcelot, Launcelot Guinevere and Guinevere
Arthur, so that no other end to the situation other than the death of
all three is possible. Hamlet increasingly dominates Claudius, but
Claudius dominates Gertrude and Gertrude, as Hamlet's mother,
dominates him. In *A Midsummer Night's Dream*, a girl is shown
breaking the bond of subordination to her father out of love for, and
a certain desire to be subordinate to, a man. Cordelia is caught
between the truth and subordination, and in asserting the truth she
traps herself in a battle for dominance with her father.

Affective and occupational

While occupational movement differs in off-stage life from affective
movement in that occupational movement carries no necessary
emotional charge with it, on stage both share the property of being
indexical, whether of state of mind or of social and political status.
For the performer, the representation of occupational movement
may well be more difficult to effect than affective movement, since
the former is likely to be far less familiar to him than the latter.
David Storey sets *The Changing Room* in a Rugby League
home-team changing-room, the actors being required to represent
the movements and behavioural mannerisms of members of the
team. Occupational movement of a different kind is demanded by
Wagner in *Siegfried*, for Siegfried is required to reforge the magic
sword Notung on stage.

Natural and mechanical

The political issue of the nature of work and the role of the worker
colours the dialectic of affective and occupational movement. In
Marxism–Leninism, a central precept is the alienation of the
worker, both from the fruits of his labour and also, by consequence,
from political or personal power. This alienation cannot but affect
the whole behaviour of the oppressed. The industrial worker seems
to move mechanically, to be a part of a dehumanised, robotic
process of regulated movement. The worker moves at the speed
and in the manner dictated by the machine. By contrast, the
emancipated worker moves naturally, even at work.

Individual and ensemble

Greek tragedy is the theatrical form most associated with chorus, and we know from Aristotle that tragedy probably developed out of choric dance, as one, then two and finally three main protagonists started to speak and move independently of the chorus itself. In Aristotle's view, the fact that a chorus is composed of, probably, fifteen individuals does not mean that they are to be viewed as fifteen distinct identities: 'The Chorus too should be regarded as one of the actors; it should be an integral part of the whole, and share in the action, in the manner not of Euripides but of Sophocles.'[1] Aristotle objects to choruses which have no direct part in the plot. He would have been more than happy with T. S. Eliot's use of choruses in his verse plays, but perhaps slightly less so with the wider-ranging speeches of Shakespeare's Chorus in *Henry V*.

The most striking Shakespearian uses of ensemble as a counterpoise to individual movement are violent. The mob in the Forum scene in *Julius Caesar* is whipped by Mark Antony into a frenzy, finally bursting into action with the tearing to pieces of Cinna the poet in mistake for Cinna the conspirator. Hector, in *Troilus and Cressida*, is executed by the awesome power of the Myrmidons, whose chilling efficiency seems more menacing than the untamed anger of the mob. Controlled ensemble movement is the basis of battle scenes, such as in the closing sequence of *Richard III* or Act IV of *Antony and Cleopatra*, in which the strength, or failing, of one man is mirrored in the state of the morale of his troops. In *Cymbeline*, the intervention of old Morgan and his two sons, Guiderius and Arviragus, dramatically turns the tide in the battle between the Britons and the Romans.

But ensembles are not necessarily violent: when King Lear first enters his court, it is in procession, and courtly scenes such as this gain in grandeur and dignity from the extent to which the courtly ensemble shows by size, sumptuousness and respect the status of the sovereign. Lear's fall is shown, to devastating effect, by the rapid shrinking of his entourage. Processions may be for more joyous occasions, as before or after weddings, but also for the solemn funerals which open *Richard III* and close *Hamlet*.

Another ensemble function is that of on-stage audience. The Women of Canterbury watch helplessly as the martyrdom of Thomas Beckett unfolds. The men of Thebes appeal to Oedipus to do something about the plague, thinking him to be their saviour; then they throw him out when they discover he is the cause of their suffering. In such a role, the spectator can only react; he has no power to initiate action. Their powerlessness is not without irony, however, because, the more Oedipus and Thomas find out, the less individual power they are shown to have.

The commonest use of a chorus in twentieth-century theatre has been in musicals, the chorus line even becoming the subject of one of the most successful of all such works, *A Chorus Line*. This show made the chorus of dancing beauties into the main plot by making their struggle for success into the *agon*, or action. It constitutes a nice reversal of Aristotelian priorities. Often, however, the link between chorus routines and plot is tenuous, though, as the popularity of Busby Berkeley's musicals demonstrates, no one seems to care. In direct contrast, Peter Terson's *Zigger Zagger* takes the seemingly inchoate energy of the football terrace and channels it through a single fan, giving a modern insight into the extent to which individual action is determined by collective forces.

Ironically, even the disorder and rowdiness of a staged football terrace has to be carefully structured and rehearsed, and the hardest directorial problem of all is making a large chorus seem spontaneous and natural in its behaviour. Most directors content themselves with choruses that form if not serried ranks then neatly symmetrical shapes and patterns of movement. A few directors, Franco Zeffirelli in particular, have a remarkable talent for crowd scenes, in which the individual action is counterpointed against a crowd that is not merely an amorphous mass but a group of other potential individuals. The audience is made to feel that any of the performers on stage could be the focus of our attention, and hence that the ones who are stand as representatives of those who are not.

Improvised and choreographed

Zeffirelli's crowd scenes are not danced, but they may accurately be described as choreographed, precisely in that they are precisely and minutely rehearsed. Yet the point of the rehearsal is to enable the performers to act spontaneously and naturally in role. The practical problem any crowd scene poses is that, the larger the performing group, the more difficult it is to create the illusion of spontaneity as opposed to the reality of chaos. In these terms, scenes such as the death of Cinna the poet, torn to bits by the angry mob in *Julius Caesar*, are the most demanding, since spontaneous anger and explosive movement have to be approached through rehearsal. Behind this apparent paradox of rehearsed spontaneity lies another of greater substance: that the purpose of all choreography, all structured movement, is to enable the performer to improvise, to move with complete freedom and ease. Through form and rule the performer proceeds to what Schiller describes as the 'formless form' of improvised play.

This *interpretative* view of improvisation, as the freedom reached through rehearsal, is distinct from the *originative* improvisation that emerged strongly during the happening movement of the 1960s. Happenings are antipathetic to rehearsal and disciplined repetition and seek a performance equivalent of Wordsworthian spontaneous overflow of powerful feeling. Erroneously appealing to such older forms as the *commedia dell'arte* as a model, such improvisation takes themes chosen at random, even called out by the audience, as the basis of performance. In fact the *commedia* performer improvises within both a strong tradition of performance, rehearsed for centuries and passed down in a highly structured form, and within established units of action or *lazzi*, which require the performer to create an interpretation of a known theme. The energy of the performance derives from the interaction of individual expression with an expressive tradition, Columbina's movements, for example, being a synthesis of Columbina's and her performer's.

Many plays have choreographed dances within them. These may range in seriousness from the Bergomaske performed at the end of *A Midsummer Night's Dream* by the Mechanicals to the brilliant tarantella that signals the beginning of Nora's new life in *A Doll's House*. The effect of the dance choreography is to create a dialectic between unchoreographed and choreographed movement equivalent to the verbal dialectic of verse and prose. Verse and dance share a common concern with rhythm, whereas prose is closer to the arhythmic nature of everyday movement. Significantly, however, a major influence on Laban's theory of movement derived from his study of occupational movement, and he perceived a vital connection between the discipline of dance and that of conveyor-belt manufacture. By applying the principles of choreography to the work environment, it was possible to improve the working-conditions of many factory workers.

One of the principal uses of the relationship between choreography and stage movement is the stage fight, which combines fencing with the precision and control of a complex dance. Sixteenth-century English actors were notable fencers, and in 1592 a fencing-school in Strasbourg had to close for a while when a troupe of English Comedians spoiled its trade by their skills.[2] Nineteenth-century actors such as Irving were also great fencers, and the epic stage duel lived on well into the Hollywood fights of Erroll Flynn and co. Anarchic versions of such fights, requiring equal discipline and control though with the opposite audience effect, are the staple fare of clowns.

Regular and irregular

While our instinctual sense is to regard natural movement as irregular and free, in contrast to mechanical movement as regular and constricting, in fact many specialised human activities deliberately regularise movement into set patterns and rhythms. Group activity of any kind, from work on a chain gang to ballroom dancing, is made easier by an express rhythm. Rhythm relieves effort through regularity. Sailors sing slow firm rhythms for hauling up the sails, Volga boatmen 'yo-heave-ho' in imitation of the rhythm of their oars. Soldiers march to 'Colonel Bogey' and attack to 'Lillibulero'. But even the more obviously natural forms of expression depend on rhythm, if of a less regular kind.

Rhythmic speech calls for a sense of rhythm in movement, even if that rhythm is not as regular as the verse it complements. In the first place, this means regular breathing, the performer knowing when and where to breathe, and using the physical rhythm of inhalation and exhalation as a part of the process of conveying meaning and feeling to the audience. They in turn will start to breathe synchronously. In the second place, subtler rhythms in the language will be reflected in the varying speed and nature of facial expression and gesture.

Common to both regular and irregular movement is the relationship between rhythm, balance and co-ordination. To create a sustained, stamping rhythm for example, as in many stomping dances, the body has to be exactly balanced and co-ordinated. Any imbalance or malco-ordination is immediately translated into a false rhythm. Physical balance and mental balance are closely allied in this, and it is, for example, a combination of mental and physical factors which generates slurred speech. Shakespeare translates his awareness of the interdependence of mental and physical balance into the sufferings of Othello, whose physical fit is accompanied by a collapse in his speech: 'It is not words that shake me thus – pish! nose, ears and lips. Is't possible? Confess. Handkerchief. O devil' (*Othello*, iv.i.42–3). When Othello falls to the ground it is in such contrast to his heroic domination of his own ground in the opening scenes that the effect is devastating.

This incident brings us back to the question of the relationship of the performer to his ground, a relationship commonly defined as *centring*. The performer both personally and in role has to find a relationship with his own physical centre and reflect that physical relationship in mental centredness. He may then be required to *decentre*, deliberately to lose balance and equilibrium, in the enactment of his role. Uncertain balance, faltering or staggering steps suggest weakness or vulnerability. Antony bestrides the world like a Colossus at first, and is hauled up in the air like a sack of grain at the last. The performer has to find a physical and a mental means to reflect this simultaneous physical and mental transformation.

Conscious and unconscious

Because stage movement is largely rehearsed, it all appears to be conscious, and, for this very reason, improvisation has been regarded as a means of establishing contact with the unconscious, instinctual self in performance. Performing unconscious moves on stage is extremely taxing – Lady Macbeth's sleep-walking scene, for example, being notoriously hard to perform plausibly. But it would be fallacious to believe that, because movements are rehearsed, they are therefore performed in a wholly conscious manner. In the first place, under the stress of performing to an audience, performers frequently draw on unconscious patterns of movement to complement the structure absorbed in rehearsal. In the second, accidents or chance inspirations frequently cause changes in rehearsed moves which not only affect the scene in which they occur but also have an incremental effect on the whole of the rest of the action. This is hardly surprising: the performer does not stop being himself on stage, and whatever influences there are active on him at a given time will contribute to the psychological condition out of which his interpretation arises.

Intended and involuntary

The relationship between the intended and the involuntary is more familiar in linguistic slips of the tongue than in movement, but there are one or two classic instances of involuntary movements betraying states of mind in an either amusing or painful way. Malvolio is a case in point. Duped into thinking that Olivia nurses a secret passion for him, he muses on a letter, dropped in his path. He fantasises a new life, no longer a steward but a lord, but the steward in him will out: 'I frown the while, and perchance wind up my watch, or play with my – some rich jewel . . .' (*Twelfth Night*, II.v.55–7). The involuntary gesture towards his chain of office betrays him more devastatingly than anything he says. Involuntary physical mannerisms frequently provide a clue in detective stories to a dissembling villain's true identity.

Sound

Sound and silence

There are two types of silence in performance: neutral and expressive. The convention of silence falling on an audience as the house lights dim has no specific meaning. The choice or imposition of silence in the course of an action is uniquely powerful. It is perhaps in music that the conscious use of silence is most impressive, as for example between the 'Crucifixus' and 'et resurrexit' of Bach's B Minor Mass. But theatrical performance uses the power of silence in a wide variety of ways.

Harold Pinter's plays are constructed around often lengthy pauses, silence being the building-brick of his dramatic architecture:

> LENNY *walks into the room from U[pstage] L[eft]. He stands. He wears pyjamas and dressing-gown. He watches* TEDDY.
>
> TEDDY *turns and sees him.*
>
> *Silence.*

TEDDY. Hullo, Lenny.
LENNY. Hullo, Teddy.

Pause.

TEDDY. I didn't hear you come down the stairs.
LENNY. I didn't.

Pause. (*The Homecoming*, I)[3]

The pause and the deliberate silence have rightly become Pinter's trademark.

One of the most potent dramatic silences comes in *Danton's Death*: Danton leaves Paris for one brief scene, in the centre of which is an agonising, and potentially endless, silence:

> I won't go any further. I won't break the stillness with the chatter of my steps and the wheezing of my breath. (*He sits down. Pause.*) Someone told me of an illness that destroys one's memory. Death must be something like that. (II.iv)[4]

In this sequence, Büchner makes the silent immobility of Danton the centre of the whole dramatic action. Silence is a traditional emblem of death. Hamlet signals his death with the ambiguous remark 'the rest is silence'; Hermione, by contrast, signals her resurrection in *The Winter's Tale* by speaking again. There is a natural metaphoric affinity between dying and leaving the stage.

Watchers, such as Troilus in the Greek camp, are frequently enjoined to be silent, and Polonius the silent watcher pays with his life for suddenly rustling behind the arras. Perhaps the most devastating breach of silence by a watcher is made by the dumb Kattrin in Brecht's *Mother Courage*. The Imperial army is about to surprise the Protestant city of Halle. Kattrin understands the plan and leaps up on the roof of an outlying cottage, banging the drum in warning:

> *Kattrin sits on the roof and begins to beat the drum that she had just previously taken out from under her apron.*

PEASANT WOMAN. Jesus, what's she doing?

PEASANT.   She's gone mad.
PEASANT WOMAN.   Get her down, quick. . . .

Kattrin stares into the distance at the city and goes on drumming. (xi)[5]

The drum becomes the voice Kattrin has never had.

Silence need not be serious in intent: Harpo Marx developed his character out of silence, and in Ben Jonson's play *Epicoene: or the Silent Woman* his precursor, Mute, is used in various witty ways:

> MOROSE (*to* MUTE).   Answer me not by speech, but by silence; unless it be otherwise (MUTE *makes a leg*) – very good . . . answer me not but with your leg, unless it be otherwise; if it be otherwise, shake your head, or shrug.   (II.i)[6]

Then, having worked Morose into frenzy of frustration, Mute re-enters and speaks. This is prelude to the more elaborate joke of the miracle of a 'silent' woman, Epicoene, who turns out in fact not to be a woman at all.

Natural and mechanical

The dialectic of sound and silence contains another binary opposition, natural and mechanical. The human voice and related natural sounds such as dogs barking, birds singing, wind, rain and thunder are counterpoised against the mechanically produced sounds of motors and tools. The aesthetic synthesis of machine and nature is the performance of music on an instrument, human skill eliciting sound from the machine. But mechanical sound is often seen as a threatening intrusion in the natural world, both because of its volume and because of its sound as such.

Until the invention of recording-techniques, all sounds, including those generated mechanically, had to be live, though machines and mechanical devices have long been used to create 'natural' effects, such as birdsong, thunder or rain. Now, the tendency is to record and mechanically reproduce even sounds that could be performed live. Cost and practicality are factors in this trend, but there is a danger that the performer's live skills are neglected as a result. Microphones and synthesisers are there to aid the performer, not to replace him at the aesthetic centre of performance.

Amplified or non-amplified

The problem of mechanical versus natural sound is at its most complex when the voice itself is being amplified, an issue which splits performers into two groups, those who approve and those who do not. Those who approve argue that audiences hear better and performers are under less strain. Those who disapprove argue that amplification turns the live voice itself into a sound effect, making the sound-engineer rather than the performer the true artist. Pop and rock music, inconceivable without amplification and engineering brilliance, could be justly criticised on those grounds, although performing to huge audiences without amplification would be nonsensical. In the theatre the issue is more finely balanced: under the influence of pop, musicals use amplified sound for the vocal numbers, but then often switch back to non-amplified speech, with disconcerting consequences. In many modern theatres, the acoustic is so poor that amplification is a necessity; yet this can also become a convenient excuse for stage performers to neglect their vocal skills, which even in the context of amplification are of primary importance.

An equivalent problem comes up in opera, where there is no assistance to the voice, for singers risk either vocal strain or becoming excessively heavy in order to create the vocal resonance required by heroic roles. Many Brünnhildes are marvellous to listen to but extremely implausible to look at, at least in as far as they are supposed to be lissom young beauties. Many 'young' tenors are middle-aged and richly endowed round the waist. This problem has no bearing on opera when merely listened to, but, as has been shown by television opera, which can so easily overcome the problem of audibility, under certain circumstances amplifying the voice may be preferable to being faced with congruity of voice but incongruity of physique for a given role.

Verbal and non-verbal

One of man's most sophisticated skills is the use of a sound system to convey linguistic meaning, speech. Though there is a performance genre, mime, that does without speech, speech is nevertheless the most sophisticated and complex single tool at the performer's disposal. The sophisticated and complex single tool at the performer's disposal. The sophistication lies partly in the cognitive complexity of language acquisition, the rules of grammar and syntax, the psychology and sociology of linguistic use, and partly in the psycho-motoric subtlety of articulating sound. Performers do not have to understand in depth how these processes work in order to be able to use them. Yet the extent to which the 'voice' is a measure of the whole person must make all performers especially concerned to master vocal skills.

The skill of speech has three aspects, the physiological, the affective and the cognitive, each of which takes a long time to learn relative to other bodily skills. On the one hand, we have to learn how to use our breathing, vocal chords, mouths and tongues to make sounds; on the other, we have to learn how to relate sound and tone to meaning. Each language solves this latter problem in a different way, and within even a single linguistic area there are wide divergences in the phonetic composition of a given word. Mastery of the sound system of received standard English does not even guarantee the user the ability to understand all English-language dialects within the British Isles. But speech is not merely the generation of sounds; it concerns the complex interaction of sound and silence that enables the listener to discern individual words, to mark the ends of phrases and statements, to interpret the tone of the voice and to make up for any syntactical or lexical gaps in the speaker's *utterance*. It connects with the complementary use of the face and body in expression, the success of an utterance being often as dependent on physical as on verbal expression.

COGNITIVE SKILLS AND COMMUNICATION THEORY
For communication to take place between two people, and hence between performers and audiences, a number of preconditions have to be met. Most obviously, they need to be able to see and/or hear each other. Ideally, they should speak the same language, and share similar sets of assumptions about the meanings of the words they use. Their gestural and microgestural systems should be compatible. But even when such preconditions are met there are still many factors which will prejudice perfect communication, and these factors are known as *noise*. Noise refers to any impairment of a *signal* – the signal being the encoded information transmitted from *A* to *B*.

In order that a communication take place between *A* and *B*, *A*'s message to *B* has to be *encoded* into a signal (such as sound or movement) and this signal must then be transmitted. In the case of the human performer, the signal is transmitted by means of the voice, generating sound waves, and the body, making movements visible by light. The signal must then be received by someone or something capable of *decoding* into a message the information reaching the ear and the eye.

However accurately a communicator expresses himself, however good the acoustic and optical conditions for performance, noise is inevitable. Indeed, most playwrights interested in the way language works deliberately exploit noise as a part of the performance art. At one level, this means using devices such as puns and *double entendres* to create deliberate insecurity in the audience as to what meaning, what message, is intended by the performer. Audiences thus have to make up their own minds about what to make of what they see and hear, which is what Shakespeare explicitly states he wishes them to do. But there are also unintentional levels of noise, caused by coughs in the auditorium, tube trains rumbling away underneath, bits of scenery falling down: all these can affect the signal being transmitted, and force the audience to compensate in their own minds for a gap in the information transmitted to them.

In fact, such gaps are no more than extreme versions of what occurs in any communication act, and all forms of human interaction depend heavily on the ability of the receiver of information to compensate by a complex process of *inference* for failings in the signal he is receiving. From the many possible ways of interpreting the meaning of even quite simple sentences, the audience have to infer what was probably meant and complement the signal with information supplied from their own memories and experience. Yet, as each individual will have a different set of memories and experiences on which to draw, the complementation process will be marginally different in each individual's mind.

When, therefore, Cordelia says, 'What shall Cordelia speak? Love and be silent', it is not merely the actress who has to make a decision as to how to speak the line: it is also up to the audience to decide whether or not to accept the interpretation transmitted by the actress, or whether to compensate for perceived failures of transmission by interpreting the line in a wholly different way. Because audiences can resist the interpretations offered them by performers if they do not believe they are what was truly intended, performers themselves are under considerable pressure to find an

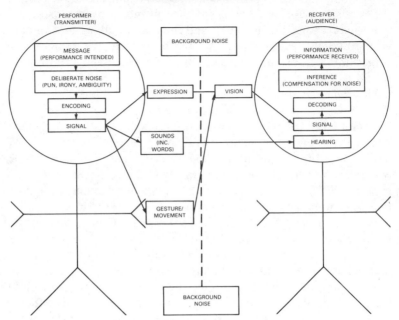

PERFORMING AS COMMUNICATION

equivalent in performance style to the negative capability of their
written scripts: that is, a performance style which leaves as open as
possible what the scene might mean.

Communication will also be affected by the psychological and
sociological patterning of the speakers. A speaker's class,
education, belief system, age, and so on, will all influence his choice
of words and constructions. In classical theories of linguistic
expression, this gives rise to the theory of *decorum*, or *proper words
in proper places*. Servants talk like servants, kings like kings.
Romanticism, by contrast, sought for the voice of the common man,
though, strikingly, it produced far less theatre of merit than
classicism. In the more contemporary study of *socio-linguistics*, the
terms *sociolect* and *ideolect* describe the lexical and syntactical rules
and conventions groups of people sharing either the same class
(sociolect) of ideology (ideolect) may use. David Storey's plays show
how children move up the social scale, out of their parents' world,
and reflect their move in changes in language. Most noticeably,
parents speak in dialect, with Northern accents, while children

speak received, standard (Oxford) English in what to the parents seems a 'posh' way.

But language is not merely a measure of class and ideology: it also signals one's psychological state. As Freud became famous for detecting, linguistic disturbance may be the first sign of psychological stress. Othello's language is famous for breaking down into animal imagery as he is hounded by Iago into madness. One of the wittiest and most poignant encapsulations of this function of language as barometer of mental health is in the first act of David Storey's *Home*:

> KATHLEEN.   I don't know what you're saying half the time. You realise that.
> HARRY.   Communication is a difficult factor.
> KATHLEEN.   Say that again.[7]

Kathleen's reply is perfectly ambiguous, perfectly poised between comprehension and madness.

The *double entendre*, or homophonic pun, is a common source of verbal humour. The Marx Brothers mastered this art to perfection:

> HAMMER.   Now here is a little peninsula, and here is a viaduct leading over to the mainland.
> CHICO.   Why a duck?
> HAMMER.   I'm all right. How are you. I say here is a little peninsula, and here's a viaduct leading over to the mainland.
> CHICO.   All right. Why a duck?   (*Cocoanuts*)[8]

This form of humour is perennial. Aristophanes has characters misapprehending and misusing words, and Sheridan gave the word malapropism to the language as a result of the linguistic errors of Mrs Malaprop (*mal à propos*).

PSYCHO-MOTORIC

Each voice is unique and unfalsifiable, which places an ineluctable physiological constraint on the empathetic powers of the performer. No matter how much he may enter into his role, his voice will always be his own, and therefore a representational instrument. Indeed, the very uniqueness of the voice means that outstanding exponents of vocal skills, such as John Gielgud or

Richard Burton, are known instantly by their voices, whatever role they are playing. What makes both so remarkable is not what they say, but how, in sonoric terms, they say it.

In analysing the *signal* generated by the voice, there are three main categories to consider: *sound*, *pitch* and *intensity*. The nature of the signal will be influenced by a large number of factors: (1) the language, or dialect spoken; (2) the specific words used; (3) the age and sex of the speaker; (4) the degree of tension in the speaker: (5) the purpose behind the signal; (6) the acoustic environment in which the signal is transmitted.

AFFECTIVE SKILLS

I have drawn a distinction between the cognitive and the psycho-motoric aspects of speech: mediating between them, and therefore at the centre of all stage speech, is affective uses of language. While on stage we are interested to hear facts that move the plot along, it is the reactions of characters to news, to situations and to states of feeling that most concern us. Even in the theatre of ideas, ideas are given significance by being shown to affect characters in emotional as well as intellectual ways. Hamlet's dilemma is not merely a cognitive speculation on guilt and the afterlife: it is at the heart of his person.

It is in the area of affective language that the boundary between verbal and non-verbal sound becomes blurred. Gasps of surprise, screams of horror, pain or delight are non-verbal sounds but take meaning within the verbal domain and may have far greater dramatic impact than speech itself. My favourite moment in the whole of the dramatic repertoire, the statue scene in *Winter's Tale*, hangs not on a word, but a gasp of amazement. Leontes touches Hermione expecting her to be cold, and he suddenly says, 'O, she's warm.' This 'O' seems to be the simplest summary of theatre's purpose Shakespeare found.

Kattrin's drumming is a classic instance of the use of non-verbal sound to convey the equivalent of a verbal message, in this case warning. But there are other kinds of *vocalised* sound – sound made by the human voice – which help put in context the verbal processes of staged speech. These range in nature from the great mob shouts of *Julius Caesar*, I.ii, where Brutus is persuaded more by the shouts than by Cassius to join the conspirators, to the 'hey nonny no' – like choruses of many songs.

Rhythmic and a-rhythmic

Rhythms in speech benefit us in two distinct ways. They help us remember things, especially when assisted by other devices such as rhyme, alliteration and assonance. And they make work easier, many songs, such as shanties or marches, having a specific work-related rhythm. Children learn rhythmic speech, through nursery rhymes and advertising jingles, quicker than the more random rhythmic patterns of everyday speech. It is easier to march 25 miles in a regulated step than to walk the same distance alone. Performers generally find it easier to commit lengthy passages of rhythmic language – to memory than to do the same with prose.

Strictly speaking, all language is rhythmic, but in performance terms there is a marked difference between verse, which is deliberately rhythmic, and prose, which is based on no obvious rhythmic pattern. John Dryden was the first to observe that the English language appears to fall easily into an *iambic* rhythm, alternating long and short syllables:

> Shall I compare thee to a summer's day?
> Thou art more lovely and more temperate.
> Rough winds do shake the darling buds of May
> And summer's lease hath all too short a date.
> (Shakespeare, Sonnet 18)

The origins of rhythm lie in nature. The human heartbeat is the basis of most binary rhythms, such as the iamb, because it alternates long and short, diastolic and systolic, pulses. But not all natural rhythms work in units of two. Galloping horses, for example, generate triadic rhythms such as *anapaests* and *dactyls*, which very occasionally figure in stage speech, and a little more often in poetry:

> The Assyrian came down like the wolf on the fold,
> And his cohorts were gleaming in purple and gold,
> And the sheen of their spears was like stars on the sea,
> When the blue wave rolls nightly on deep Gallilee.
> (Lord Byron, 'The Siege of Sennacherib')[9]

Such rhythms evoke speed and quickening energy.

Organised into blocks, rhythms are known as *metres*, units of poetic measure. Metres are made up of *feet*, the building sections of a poetic line. The commonest metre in English-language drama is the *iambic pentameter*, lines of five *bi-syllabic* feet, alternating five long (marked ‾) and five short (marked ˘) syllables. The Shakespeare sonnet I quote above is in just such iambic pentameters. Contrasted against the relative solidity of the iambic pentameter area whole range of shorter lines, still largely iambic in structure, but with a lighter, more tripping feel:

> Where the bee sucks, there suck I;
> In a cowslip's bell I lie;
> There I couch when owls do cry.
> On the bat's back I do fly
> After summer merrily.
> Merrily, merrily shall I live now
> Under the blossom that hangs on the bough.
>
> (*Tempest*, v.i.88–94)

The rhythm catches exactly Ariel's mercurial personality. Classical French drama by contrast works in hexameters, known as *alexandrines*, lines of six feet, which are more stately (some would argue, more ponderous) than the English iambic line.

While the iambic pentameter has five feet, it tends to have only four *stresses*, (marked ´), syllables which the voice is intended to accent. There are two reasons for this. The first is a natural desire for symmetry, the ear preferring to hear two half-lines in balance, the balance being reinforced by the meter. The second is the history in English of the *alliterative long line*, the basis of Anglo-Saxon and much medieval poetry, which worked on a principle of stress and alliteration rather than metre, a concept more classical in origin. In our own century, T. S. Eliot achieved remarkable success in creating a contemporary version of the stressed line in *Murder in the Cathedral*:

> Dóes the bírd síng in the Sóuth?
> Only the séa-bird críes, driven inlánd by the stórm.
> Whát sígn of the spríng of the yéar?
> Only the déath of the óld: not a stír, not a shóot, not a bréath.
>
> (II)[10]

The fifth stress in the final line of the quotation marks it as especially significant to the ear, pointing up 'stir', 'shoot' and 'breath'.

Rhythm assists performers in a technical way by giving them indications of where to take breaths, and how to phrase and structure speeches. There is a natural break at the end of a line of verse, often reinforced by a punctuation mark. Even if the performer does not breathe at these points, there is commonly a very brief pause in speech to indicate to the ear that the line has ended. Well-trained performers will, if necessary, be able to speak eight iambic lines without a breath. Commonly, however, there will be shorter units of delivery, perhaps four lines or a couplet long, after which a breath is a natural indicator of a sense break.

Occasionally, to vary the rhythm and to break what Ezra Pound called the 'tyranny of the iambic pentameter', there will be an *enjambement*, when the voice is deliberately made to carry over from one line to the next without pause or *end-stop*. This will then have a knock-on effect of tripping the listener out of what may be a soporific adaptation to a single beat. In *Volpone*, Ben Jonson nails his rhythmic colours firmly to the mast by breaking the end-stop convention in the opening speech:

> VOLPONE.   Good morning to the day; and next, my gold! –
> Open the shrine that I may see my saint.

> MOSCA *withdraws the curtain, and discovers piles of gold, plate, jewels etc.*

> Hail the world's soul and mine, more glad than is
> The teeming earth to see the long'd for sun
> Peep through the horns of the celestial Ram,
> Am I to view thy splendour darkening his;
> That lying here amongst my other hoards
> Shew'st like a flame by night, or like the day
> Struck out of chaos, when all darkness fled
> Unto the centre.
>
>   (I.i)[11]

The strong break in the middle of the last line of the quotation, reinforced by the full stop, makes us hear the word 'centre' with particular emphasis. This technique of cutting the line is known as *caesura*, literally named after Julius Caesar, who was famed for being cut from his mother's womb. Caesuras may be of two kinds: *strong* (as here after the second foot) and *weak* (as after the third). Most lines have a caesura, even if the punctuation does not make this explicit. Volpone's line 'Open the shrine that I may see my saint', breaks into two halves between 'shrine' and 'that', the word 'that' acting as punctuation by opening a relative clause.

Variations in the iambic pentameter may be achieved by two main devices, the *inversion* of a foot, or the addition of one extra syllable, the *hypermetric* foot. In the line 'Open the shrine that I may see my saint', Jonson inverts the opening foot, so that both the long syllable and the stress fall on the 'o' sound. This interrupts the regularity of the first half of the line. In Hamlet's most celebrated soliloquy, Shakespeare deceives the ear in the very first line, by adding one extra syllable: 'To be, or not to be: that is the question.' He also balances the line around a weak caesura, after the third foot, so paradoxically putting the most complex of all human questions in the context of a 'weak' metrical shape. Nor is this his only trick, for the performer has to decide where to put the stresses, whether to stress 'be', 'not' and 'be' in the first half line, or, if not, which stress to leave out. Likewise, in the second half of the line, the voice will naturally run 'is' and 'the' together, to retain the metrical shape, leaving 'that' and 'ques-' as the stressed syllables. By running 'is' and 'the' together, the performer would be making the rhythm *sprung* – a term, though not a technique, introduced by the poet Gerard Manley Hopkins.[12] Sprung rhythm permits a variable number of unstressed syllables after a stressed syllable, within the overall shape of the ordered metre. So within a pentameter containing sprung rhythm there are still five feet, and four stresses, but more than ten syllables:

> The New Year waits, breathes, waits, whispers in darkness.
> While the labourer kicks off a muddy boot and stretches his hand
>   to the fire,
> The New Year waits, destiny waits for the coming. . . . .
>   (*Murder in the Cathedral*, 1)[13]

One potential benefit of such a line is that it allows a more naturalistic approximation to human speech while retaining the motor energy of specific rhythmic and stress rules.

Probably because none of us speaks verse in everyday conversation, except for the occasional, accidental rhyme, we regard verse as much harder to write than prose. But this is not necessarily the case. Shakespeare is best known for his deliberate modulation between verse and prose. In the earlier works, this is associated with differences between high-life characters, who speak verse, and low-life, who speak prose. But, as his writing developed, he turned more to a blend of verse and prose that had less obvious class strategy about it, suggesting that he probably found the writing of verse easier than prose precisely because the rules of composition, which appear on the outside so forbidding, actually, once mastered, are a great help. Ibsen, perhaps provocatively, argued that he turned in mid-career from verse to prose because writing prose was more difficult, which would confirm that the benefits of rhythm accrue to writers as well as performers in the execution of their craft.

Rhythm is the chief connecting-agent between speech and music, on the one hand, and speech and movement, on the other. It is a natural step to move from rhythmic speech to rhythmic singing – to the song. It is equally natural to respond to rhythm by movement, so that the structures of dance and those of poetry are based on similar rhythmic principles. I have found it easier to approach the rudiments of speaking Shakespeare's verse through movement rather than through technical elucidation of the iambic pentameter, which makes a good deal more sense once the concept of rhythm itself has been explained.

Conscious and instinctive

While the bulk of what we say is designed to convey information, or to make something happen, it is implicit in expressions such as Leontes's 'O' that there are sounds which are made instinctively. We do not consciously decide to say 'ouch' when we stub our toes, or scream when we see something horrible and unexpected; the sounds just come. The problem for the performer is that, in a dramatic situation requiring this sort of instinctive response, he will know in advance what is required and have great difficulty, therefore, in being convincingly instinctive. When Imogen wakes up next to a headless body, she is understandably distressed. When the actress wakes up next to a headless dummy for the fiftieth time, shock may be the last thing on her mind. Likewise, Shakespeare gives the performer playing Lady Macbeth a doubly taxing task by requiring her to feign feigning shock at Duncan's murder. The task the performer therefore faces is the realistic portrayal of the obviously artificial, how consciously to represent instinctive responses.

Dramatists are not unaware of this difficulty and offer one conscious linguistic trick to help. I suggested above that the performer might run together 'is' and 'the' at the start of Hamlet's soliloquy. But clearly there is a case for stressing 'the', since 'To be or not to be' might well be regarded as *the* question. In this case we should have to make a rhythmic accommodation elsewhere in the line. The effect of this uncertainty in the stress is to widen the number of possible interpretations the performer could offer for the line, and so make it much more likely that on a given night a spontaneous decision between various options, giving at least the illusion of instinctive response, will be made. In *King Lear* for example, Cordelia has to decide how to say one of the most ambiguous lines Shakespeare conceived: 'What shall Cordelia speak? Love and be silent' (i.i.61). The moment is one of acute psychological stress for the character, and, by the very difficulty of the decision how to say the line, Shakespeare aids the actress in achieving a sense of frustrated shock at being called on to speak to such a question.

Intended and involuntary

In many respects this category overlaps with the previous one, except in the problem of the *lapsus linguae*, or slip of the tongue. The disturbed unconscious may well play a trick on the conscious mind by causing the speaker to intend one word but involuntarily utter another. The relative frequency with which performers lapse unconsciously from their lines into unconscious preoccupations of their own is a clear sign of the interaction of the competing realities off- and on-stage in which they live. Creating a genuine *lapsus linguae* within role, however, is a technical feat of extreme ability.

Pitched and unpitched

The distinction between pitched and unpitched sound, while of special significance in distinctions between performance genres, such as that between a play and an opera, is problematic. First, as Ezra Pound pointed out,[14] all poetic language seems to imply a hidden music; and, secondly, the voice, even when talking, is itself pitched. In plays, pitched sound is used for three main purposes, as *song*, as *effect* and as *underscore*, each of which breaks the surface of spoken sound. *Music drama* and its associated genre the *musical* have a more even balance of pitched and unpitched sound, the action itself being advanced through musical scenes, especially love songs and duets. *Opera* is pitched throughout, as was classical Greek tragedy, which should perhaps be understood in terms of opera.

Song

The song is the densest and most complex stage sound, being simultaneously pitched verbal and vocal. No device has been more favoured by dramatists than the song for varying the nature of performance sound, while at the same time offering rhythmic and tonal counterparts to the dialogue. So significant was singing to the actor in the late sixteenth century that the Elizabethan actor was as much a singer as a speaker, and the Fools in particular had a repertoire of songs and sung interludes, called jigs. The songs would often be melancholy, as Amiens's song in *As You Like It*:

> Blow, blow thou winter wind
> Thou art not so unkind
>   As man's ingratitude.
> Thy tooth is not so keen,
> Because thou art not seen,
>   Although thy breath be rude.

Yet, even in moments of melancholy, there is, at least rhythmically, a jauntier counterpoise, as in Amiens's chorus:

> Heigh-ho, sing heigh-ho unto the green holly.
> Most friendship is feigning, most loving mere folly.
>   Then heigh-ho, the holly.
>   This life is most jolly.

>   (II.vii.174–83)

Most commonly, however, Shakespeare uses a balladic melody and
rhythm to create a tension between the beauty of the sound and the
pain of the content:

> When that I was and a little tiny boy,
>   With hey, ho, the wind and the rain
> A foolish thing was but a toy,
>   For the rain it raineth every day.
>   (*Twelfth Night*, v.i.375–9)

This simple but effective device has been much imitated and even
developed. Bertolt Brecht regarded the shift between song and
speech as one of the most important aspects of his stagecraft,
intrinsic to the *alienation effect* he sought to achieve. In *Mother
Courage*, for example, there are frequent interruptions of the
'story' for songs – 'The Song of the Great Capitulation', 'The Song
of the Hours' – in which characters are made to sing songs that
extend or even contradict what we have previously seen of their
character. So extensive is Brecht's use of song that in *The
Threepenny Opera* he moves, if not strictly into opera, at least into
music drama.

   Brecht's influence on modern British theatre is most visible in the
extensive use of song as an alienating, or directly political, device.
One of the loveliest moments in John Arden's *Sergeant Musgrave's
Dance* is Attercliffe's song which closes the play:

> Your blood-red rose is withered and gone
> And fallen on the floor:
> And he who brought the apple down
> Shall be my darling dear.
>
> For the apple holds a seed will grow
> In live and lengthy joy
> To raise a flourishing tree of fruit
> For ever and a day.
> With fal-la-la-the-dee, toor-a-ley,
> For ever and a day.
>   (III.ii)[15]

The lyricism is a fine counterbalance to the harsher sentiments of
the play.

Effect

The range of possible sound effects is now as great as man's capacity to generate sounds, helped by the ever-increasing sophistication of recording- and mixing-techniques. Cars are made to arrive that we never see; trains depart; police sirens wail; revolvers are fired. The principle of synecdoche enables us to construct a complete event from its most salient sonoric characteristic: the noise of a helicopter tells us in Harald Müller's *Flotsam* that a little girl has drowned, a girl we never see on stage; the pistol shot at the end of Chekhov's *Ivanov* tells us unequivocally that Ivanov has killed himself.

Such sounds are in themselves unambiguous, and depend on this unambiguity for their success. The dilemma they raise for the performer is more an aesthetic one, as to whether or not to use artificial aids in live performance, or whether to make all sounds on stage, live. Various reasons prevent this hard-line position gaining much ground. It is both expensive and impractical to route a railway line past one's theatre, and arrange exact cueing of trains, just to make convincing use of these sounds. Symphonic orchestral numbers may also break the bank of small production companies if they are to be live. Those who do not like artificial aids must, therefore, either avoid works which demand them, or replicate them with the voice.

AMBIGUOUS SOUND

More enigmatic are sounds that have a direct influence on the action without being fully clear in meaning. In *The Cherry Orchard* a sound becomes the dominant dramatic force: '*A sound is heard that seems to come from the sky, like a breaking harp-string, dying away mournfully. All is still again, and there is nothing heard but the strokes of the axe far away in the orchard*' (III).[16] The sound of the harp-string is pitched, in deliberate counterpoint to the dull sound of the axe. The axe's remoteness, however, besides indicating the destruction of the world that the orchard symbolised, lends further ambiguity to the strange noise with which the play ends. A similar use of a sound closes Ibsen's *A Doll's House*, when Nora leaves Torvald. The stage direction calls for a dull, booming sound, coming not so much from the hallway as from under the stage, as if her departure is like a moral earthquake, whose rumble we both hear and feel. Such effects are, however, singularly difficult to put into practice.

Underscoring

Certain types of scene, particularly those associated with ceremonies such as marriage or funerals, or with magic and enchantment, have traditionally been accompanied by music, a technique now known as *underscoring*. This technique is predominantly instrumental in nature. When Paulina brings Hermione back, she calls 'Music, awake her: strike' (*Winter's Tale*, v.iii). In the English Comedians' play of *The Prodigal Son* (1620) the Son directs the musicians how to play, according to his mood: '*The Musicians strike up their violins / the* SON *toasts the* DAUGHTER. . . . He holds her in his arms and kisses her.*' Then, as the Son wishes to pursue his seduction, he instructs the musicians to quieten down. The direction then reads, '*The Musicians strike up again / but play very softly, so that one can speak over the music* . . . .'[17] This rather literal use of underscoring is echoed in the many composers who have subsequently written incidental music to Shakespeare's work, such as Felix Mendelssohn-Bartholdy with his incidental music to *A Midsummer Night's Dream*. A natural extension of this takes composers into opera, as with Verdi's Shakespeare operas, *Othello*, *Falstaff* and *Macbeth*, or ballet, as in the numerous versions of *Romeo and Juliet*.

Dance music is not merely the concern of ballet, but in the sixteenth and seventeenth centuries was part of the staple fare of theatrical entertainment. English actors abroad at that time were rated as highly for their dancing-skills as for their acting-abilities. Dances also form key moments in dramatic actions. In Thomas Dekker's play *Fortunatus*, the death of Fortunatus is followed by a dance of satyrs, who come on gleefully to claim his body. In *Much Ado about Nothing*, the wooing-sequence in Act II scene i is tied up in a courtly dance.

Integrating movement and sound

In this chapter I have treated movement and sound in their constituent categories, isolating brief incidents in plays as examples of particular aspects of performance. But it is rare in performance that anything occurs in such isolation, although performance is far from being continuous in nature. In the next chapter, performance will be considered as an integrated and socially integrating art.

Chapter 6

Cheered and Checked: Performers and Audiences

Range and integration

Performance draws on a uniquely wide range of disciplines and skills: electrics, electronics, architecture, carpentry, painting, graphic and scenic design, computing (for lighting and accounting), financial management, marketing, music, acoustics, acting, dancing, singing, and so on and so forth. Yet performance is not solely about displaying range: it is also concerned with aesthetic, intellectual and social integration. It encourages the integration of theory and practice; it combines psycho-motoric, affective and cognitive learning; it unites art with technology; it bonds performers with audiences. This combination of range and integration makes it the classic humanist discipline, which is why Lord Bacon so admired it.

The process by which a single, coherent performance is constructed out of the infinite range of possibilities open to it is one analogous to classic scientific method, another factor in Bacon's admiration. Through rehearsal, interpretative hypotheses are constructed which then in rehearsal are analysed, or deconstructed. Only when a full range of possibilities has been explored is one chosen for performance, and even that choice is subject to review. This method is the way of negation, the *via negativa*. In rehearsal as in scientific experiment, solutions are conceived in the expectation that they will be unsatisfactory.

This means that the performance process operates simultaneously on two levels: the one is concrete, the choice and preparation of a work for performance of a given work to a given audience at a given time. The other is more abstract and concerns the continuous development of the overall cultural function of performance. By analogy with mathematics, performance thus generates both *pure* and *applied* skills, the pure skills being those of immediate importance to performers in the act of performing, the applied skills concerning those aspects of everyday life that most resemble theatre. In the metaphor of the world as stage the two are reintegrated, the pure skills of performing all having some equivalent in the everyday world.

Contracts with the audience

Performers enter two types of relationship with their audiences – *aesthetic* and *financial* – the two being interdependent. When someone buys a ticket to a show, he exchanges money for the expectation of aesthetic satisfaction and entertainment. When a state, or a Maecenas, supports a performer by more general subsidy, wider issues are engaged, affecting the role of the performer in society. First the aesthetic aspect to the contract.

The aesthetic contract: reception theory and practice

Performances communicate with audiences on the sensory premiss that what they do and say is seen and heard by the audience. This premiss is not to be taken for granted, however, and the first line of *Hamlet*, 'Who's there?', seems addressed as much to the audience as to the possible ghost. Within this context there are three options open to them as to how to treat the communication process, which manifest themselves in two special types of stage speech, *direct address to the audience* and *soliloquy*, which elicit special modes of listening.

Speaking and listening: direct address

Shakespeare has a habit of closing plays on direct address, the end of *Troilus and Cressida* being his most acerbic use of the device:

> As many as be here of pander's hall,
> Your eyes half out, weep at Pandar's fall;
> Or, if you cannot weep, yet give some groans,
> Though not for me, yet for your aching bones.
>
> (v.x.46–9)

In the balanced last line, Pandarus redirects the attention of the audience from himself to them.

A different form of direct address is the aside in which the audience's collusion with point of view of a particular character on stage is established. Such an aside provides the basis for the whole plot of Wycherley's *The Country Wife*, for in his opening line Horner hints at the joke he is to play on his peers: 'A quack is as fit for a pimp as a midwife for a bawd; they are still but in their way both helpers of nature . . .'(I.i).[1] The audience knows that his alleged sexual impotence is a fiction that permits Horner freedom of access to women otherwise denied him. The two examples illustrate the main functions of direct address: to provide information and to elicit sympathy for a particular character. Both Hamlet and Cordelia start their roles on asides, which establish them in the audience's favour from the start. At the same time, they illustrate the danger for the audience in the direct-address mode, the danger of accepting the character's own perspective on a problem rather than a more objective, and perhaps more moral, one. Because we are flattered by Horner's honesty, we do not stop to question whether his duplicity is something we should interest ourselves in. In a more damaging way, we allow ourselves to fall victim to Richard III's rhetoric.

Speaking and listening: soliloquy

Soliloquies are ambiguous in nature in that they seem intended to be heard by the audience as a form of direct address and yet only overheard in that there is a confessional honesty about them that makes us feel uncertain as to our right to be hearing such intimate revelations. Hamlet's 'To be or not to be' illustrates the problem well, for he delivers it in the knowledge that he is being overheard not just by an off-stage audience but also by members of the court on stage. Is his whole speech a piece of posturing for their benefit? How far are we the audience to trust what he tells us? Not the least of the relativities of performance lies in the problem of establishing what is trustworthy and what not. Only we, the audience, have the final power to decide.

These modes of speech elicit heightened attention to detail and a sense of special relationship with the speaker. Similar effects can be achieved by directing the audience to look in a particular way, or from a particular perspective.

Showing and seeing

Throughout *Othello*, Iago dedicates himself to making others, especially Othello, see things as he wants them to be seen. The result is an object lesson in image manipulation. Iago stage-manages a play for Othello which deceives him utterly. When Hamlet tries a similar device, however, he is less successful, and a comparison of the two reminds us that it is less the shower who determines the impact of what he shows than the watcher. Othello is predisposed to see what Iago wishes him to see; Claudius is rather better defended.

The complexities of perspective preoccupy Shakespeare in *Troilus and Cressida*, in the centre of which is a scene with a double perspective. Troilus and Ulysses watch Cressida and Diomedes. Watching all four is Thersites:

THERSITES.   Now the pledge; now, now, now.
CRESSIDA.   Here, Diomed, keep this sleeve.
TROILUS.   O beauty, where is they faith?
ULYSSES.   My Lord.
TROILUS.   I will be patient; outwardly I will.
CRESSIDA.   You look upon that sleeve; behold it well.
   He lov'd me – O false wench – Give't me again.   (v.ii.64–9)

The rapid change of speaking voice guides us through a rapid change in where to look and how to feel. Thersites, cynical and frustrated, wishes nothing but wars and lechery, egging Cressida on to betray Troilus. Troilus cannot believe what he sees, and Ulysses has to restrain him from intervening. Cressida is attacked by guilt, and Diomedes is puzzled. The same event, the giving of a sleeve from a woman to a man, turns out to have as many meanings as there are participants in and observers of the act. The implication for the theatrical process as a whole is clear: there is no such thing as the meaning of a scene, only a variety of interconnected meanings. How these meanings are generated is the business of reception theory.

Literary studies in the past two decades have been increasingly concerned with *reception theory*,[2] the study of the process by which meaning is generated by the reader in relationship with a text or group of texts. Oddly, little has been done to integrate this thinking with theatre analysis, in which the issue of reception is perhaps at its most sensitive and immediate. In brief, the theory suggests that communication between reader and text (and by analogy performers and audience) is only possible if their *horizons of expectation* meet. That is, unless their respective languages, beliefs and values (together constituting their *horizon of expectation*) are reasonably close, performers and audiences will not have the means of responding to one another. The theory has both a *synchronic* and a *diachronic* aspect. The synchronic study of performance looks at individual performances in front of individual audiences and attempts to assess their effect. The diachronic study looks at the wider trends of taste in performance through history, considering why certain plays and performance styles are in favour in certain epochs and out in others.

The oddness of the failure to apply reception theory to performance is that, in performance reception, audience response is at its most immediate and direct. While the author of a novel rarely directly confronts his audience, the performer is always in front of his, constantly adapting what he does in response to their reactions to him. This is reception theory in creative practice, for the performer mediates between authorial intentions and audience expectations, negotiating a way between representing the playwright to the audience and representing the audience to the playwright. True, the playwright always has the direct means of access to the audience available to him, print, but this relationship is the business of literary not performance studies.

The effect of reception theory is to shift the burden of analysis away from the authorial process of making the text to the 'making' (the poesis) that goes on in the receiver's mind. The making-process goes on in the *gaps* or *indeterminacies* of the text – that is, in those moments when the reader has to make up his own mind what to think about the information he is offered, having to complement it with knowledge and expectations of his own in order for it to make sense at all. This attention to gaps and indeterminacies constitutes a translation of the advances made in communication theory as a whole into the more limited domain of literary and theatrical study.

Instinctive tact: engagement with the audience

In his theory of warfare, *On War*,[3] Clausewitz examines what makes a good performer in battle, and his conclusion is that the good performer has two strengths: first, he is not so schooled in battles of the past that he cannot think of how to fight the battle of the present; secondly, he knows how to react, which is more important than knowing how to act. The qualities Clausewitz describes are summarised in the phrase 'instinctive tact', by which he means the ability to achieve effortlessly and instinctively whatever the situation in hand demands. This skill is not 'active' but rather 'reactive': fighting-skills have been rehearsed to a point where the fighter is capable of free improvisation upon them. Through the mastery of rules, complete freedom of mind and body are achieved.

Performance is very similar, in that the crucial test of a performer's skill is not how well he replicates what was done in rehearsal, what was done at drama school, but how well in the moment of engagement with a specific play and a specific audience he deploys his instinctive tact as performer.

In performance there are two levels of dramatic engagement. There is the on-stage conflict of forces which constitute the plot of the drama, and there is the engagement with the audience in an imaginative act of constructing a possible world. In my opening analysis of the preconditions for a performance, I deliberately omitted the audience because there are a number of difficulties about the theory of performance, which regards performance as the product of the meeting of performers with an audience.

First, the presence of real, or imagined, noise in the performers' signals creates a practical disjunction between what the performers intend and what the audience understand to be their intentions. While both may share an awareness that they are participating in a performance, what that event actually means may be subject to widely divergent interpretation. In this context, it is not the physical meeting of performers and audience which matters, but their shared consciousness of performance. This consciousness, however, is not a function of the meeting, nor is it dependent on there being an audience at all. It stems from the representational aspect of the actant, in which the performer is his own audience.

Secondly, it is not the presence of an audience which turns a 'real' event into a 'performance'. If this were the case, any street accident would be a performance, whereas there is clearly no intention to perform on the part of those who are victims of the accident. Performers state by their actions that what they are performing is simultaneously real and not real, is in effect simply 'possible'. The audience in these terms do not test the performance as such, over which they have little control, but rather test the validity of its perceived meanings within the wider context of culture as a whole.

This second problem leads directly to a third, that of defining what we actually mean by an audience. In Brecht's view, theatre is to educate the masses in a particular ideology, and in so doing incite them to action outside the theatre. In other words, performances turn audiences into performers, by making them want to go out into the street and make real that which had been presented as theatre. This perhaps narrowly Marxist view may be better understood in the context defined by Rousseau, in which the true measure of a celebratory performance was the reversal of roles by which the audience became the performance. That is, if performers succeed in their task, the audience no longer feels itself to be passive, merely watching, but senses itself to be the action, to have so fully intervened in the gaps and indeterminacies of the performance as to have broken down the distinction between the stage and the auditorium, the performer and the spectator. As long as an audience perceives itself to be an audience, rather than as passive performers, performance may be held not to have taken place. The transformational process by which an actor enters a role must be replicated in the manner in which an audience enters a performance, or no performance has occurred.

The audience's entry into a performance is through a threshold of awareness from off-stage consciousness into performance consciousness. The passage through this threshold we may call *tuning in*. I have frequently found that it takes about twenty minutes of stage time for this threshold to be crossed, and not until then am I fully tuned in to the signals being transmitted to me. Equally, once within a performance consciousness, the reverse threshold, passing from performance world into the off-stage world may take considerably longer than the fleeting moments of the curtain call, momentous performances leaving audiences in a different state of consciousness for hours or even days afterwards.

The audience is not a precondition of performance; but it is the means by which the possible world generated by the performer is mediated into the wider culture, the agent of transformation from potential to actual. If an audience are persuaded of the validity of a performance, then its messages will be transmitted by them into the wider cultural consciousness. If it is not, then these messages will be filtered out as noise. It may take some time, however, before the audience catch up with the performer, in the sense that they will need to be educated in the performer's codes in order to be able to decode them. In the short term, this is the tuning-in process already referred to; in the long term, this is part of the wider process of cultural adaptation.

Ben Jonson's awareness of the natural disjunction of interests between performers and their audiences led him to introduce a form of contract between performers and audiences at the start of *Bartholomew Fair*, in which he describes the respective duties of both sides:

> Articles of agreement, indented, between the spectators and hearers, at the Hope on the Bankside in the county of Surrey, on the one party; and the author of *Bartholomew Fair*, in the said place and county, on the other party: . . .
>   It is covenanted and agreed, by and between the parties above-said, and the said spectators and hearers . . . to remain in their places . . . for the space of two hours and an half, and somewhat more. In which time the author promiseth to present them, by us, with a sufficient play, called *Bartholomew Fair* . . .[4]

There is an implicit contract between the parties to any public performance, which, for all Jonson's irony, centres on the performers' acceptance of a duty to entertain their audience, and on the audience's preparedness to be entertained. But no contract can compel the opposing parties to the impossible, to understanding each other when the conditions for communication are not to hand. No amount of promising entertainment will guarantee its occurring; no degree of insistence on a desire to communicate will ensure that communication does take place.

Contemporary with Ben Jonson was Cervantes, in whose *Don Quixote*[5] both these difficulties are given a witty yet salutary appraisal. Don Quixote, watching a puppet show, becomes so incensed with it that he attacks the puppets with his sword. No rational appeal to his sense of fictionality will convince him that the objects of his wrath are not real. His failure to comprehend the performance is only a failure at a phenomenological level: he fails to see that the puppets merely represent the plot. Yet at a moral level they are the action they represent, and Quixote has morality on his side in his intervention. Further, Quixote's fury exposes one of the absurdities of performance: that we do not rise up and intervene when on-stage we see murderers committing murder, or adulterers breaking vows. We sit and watch, which is just the reason why Augustine so doubted the moral defence of theatre.[6]

In a different sense, Quixote becomes what Rousseau asks of all audiences to all spectacles: the true object of the spectacle. It is not the puppet play that concerns us as readers in the events Cervantes describes; but rather Quixote's reactions to it, just as in *Tom Jones*[7] it is less Garrick's performance as Hamlet that draws our attention than Partridge's response to the performance. Both Fielding, himself a playwright, and Quixote demonstrate an awareness of the disjunction between audience and performance, there being no necessary relationship between them from which a plausible definition of performance could be constructed.

Quixote's response is what Schiller describes as *naïve*,[8] the empathetic, identificatory relationship between on-stage and off-stage reality. This is what I have described as the *being* aspect of performing. Sancho Panza's amusement is equivalent to Schiller's *sentimentality*, by which he means not emotional but rather intellectual and cognitive understanding. This is what I have described as the *representational* in performance. In Schiller's view, as implicitly in Cervantes's, the ideal spectator is a complementary blend of both, a mixture of a child-like belief in what is shown and an adult recognition that it is illusion, an amalgam of empathetic belief and sympathetic observation.

Shakespeare knew that theatre depends on the active participation of the audience's mind. Asking participation of an audience has the invaluable effect of rendering easier the process of aligning theirs and the text's horizons of expectation, which is one practical reason why Shakespeare's plays have stood the test of time

so well. By contrast, the theatre of escape relieves the audience of
the burden of imaginative participation in the performance.

Changing patterns of aesthetic expectation

Since the advent of film and later television, the theatre of escape
has shifted its attention increasingly away from live performance to
electronically transmitted images over which the viewer has no
control other than literally or metaphorically to switch off. While
live performance is an interaction between audience and
performers, unique on every occasion, television and film both are
infinitely repeatable. While live performance acknowledges the
spontaneous, the unrehearsed and the improvised as the source of
constant renewal, films and videos are made once and for all on the
cutting-table or in the editing-suite. Their objective is a perfect
realisation of their shooting-script, their aesthetic determined by
the potential for aesthetic perfection implicit in a medium
composed of a potentially infinite set of 'takes'.

Marshall McLuhan distinguishes between film and theatre
according to his scale of 'hot' and 'cool'.[9] The 'hot' medium of film is
one which is simply to be received, permitting no engagement by
the audience in the making of its meanings. This is contrasted with
the 'cool' medium of theatre, which depends substantially on its
audience. McLuhan's theory identifies the principal difference
between the media, but not in a wholly acceptable way. First, even
the hot medium can be as ambiguous as the cool one; and, secondly,
he treats the medium of television as like theatre, a cool medium,
whereas it tends to pay least attention of all media to a notional
audience having any imaginative power of intervention in its
meaning. Television at its worst is crassly literal-minded.

When Shakespeare gave Bohemia a sea coast – and he surely
knew it had none – no one could go to that country with a camera
and beam back live pictures proving him wrong. Now someone can.
Our man in Bohemia stands face to camera and tells us solemnly
over steaming bowls of goulash about the terrible lack of sea coast in
Bohemia. Yet the fact that he can do so proves one of McLuhan's
contentions, that the dimensions of the world have now been
shrunk by electronic means of a communication to the point where
we live in a village, and the Live Aid concert, with its audience of
half the 'Global Village',[10] confirmed his point. The implication of

this shift in dimensions is necessarily towards literal-mindedness. For, whereas Shakespeare's claim that the world was a stage was an audacious methaphor, pre-emptively appropriating all that the world was imagined to contain for performance, the electronic Global Village is a fact we can prove by empirical observation. When Shakespeare's audience was confronted with apparent improbability, the vastness of what was still not known acted as a screen between the playwright's fantasy and the world of facts. Now, the playwright's imagination is rigorously tested against the known.

The conceptual danger of television, therefore, is that it can stultify the individual imagination by its very literal-mindedness. Naturalism becomes an obsession, accuracy not just a matter of professional pride but a working neurosis. Like Don Quixote, the viewer is constantly thought to be worried by the thought of bells ringing from mosques. Shakespeare's point in *The Winter's Tale*, as throughout his work, is that it does not matter if the off-stage Bohemia has or has not a sea coast, for what counts is the plausibility or probability of such a fact on stage, *in context*. The aesthetic correlative of theatrical probability is thus not to be sought outside performance but within it.

This has further implications for any cultural theory of television. Raymond Williams has argued for treating the television as the point of origin of the new dramaturgy,[11] and, in that his case implies the decentralisation of culture and its democratisation through mass access, it stands as a model. But the exchange of theatrical box-set for the electronic boxed set in the living-room corner is not quite that simple, since the television has not got the *back-channel* available to theatre, the ability of the audience to register an immediate response to the performer in a manner that the performer can respond to in the course of performing. True, we all shout at the television, but safe in the knowledge that only the neighbours can hear. Eventually, limited back-channel facilities will be available to television, the phone-in being perhaps the start of this integration of audience response into the medium. And it has to be admitted that theatrical performers set very narrow limits on the extent to which any direct audience intervention is possible in a live performance; only the Christmas pantomime, popular no doubt for this very reason, has an established tradition of audience engagement in the course of the action. Nevertheless, television is dominantly a recorded medium, precluding audiences intervention *de facto*. Audiences are left with one, blunt sanction: turning over, or off.

The financial contract

Productions are sometimes described as a 'critical success', which means that they received good reviews but had no audiences. Critical failures can be box-office successes. Theatre spans two value systems, aesthetic and economic, and it is now time to consider the implications of this duality in its nature, a duality echoed in the wider semantic sense of performance: a share is said to perform well on the Stock Exchange if it rises; a child's performance is good if he or she achieves high marks. Theatre's own performance is measured by a mixture of aesthetic and financial criteria.

In deciding what and how to perform, director and producer will be influenced by many non-aesthetic factors. These are (1) *size of venue*, (2) *overall financial position*, (3) *expected box-office appeal*, (4) *venue image*, (5) *political influence*, and (6) *technical facilities*.

SIZE OF VENUE

The size of the venue, in terms both of its stage dimensions and of its audience capacity, will be one of the single most significant influences on all its activities. The larger it is in proportion to its audience-catchment area, the more neutral is likely to be its artistic policy. Small venues in large cities can build up a group of regular clients, constituting in effect a club, many of whom will share social and economic characteristics. Small venues in small towns or villages will be more neutral in nature, since it will be as hard for them to attract regular audiences as for large venues in cities. Successful venues can, however, generate audiences, so that there is no absolute formula governing the size of a venue and its catchment area. A tradition of amateur theatre of a high standard, as in theatres such as the Maddermarket in Norwich, has created a size of audience for its productions larger cities cannot match.

In large cities there is a natural hierarchy of venues in relation to their size, of small scale (up to 200 seats), medium scale (200–600) and large (over 600), though these concepts are themselves variable. Small for rock concerts is 1000 seats, large 100,000.

FINANCIAL POSITION

A venue's financial ability to promote a certain kind of performance will be partly a function of its size. If a popular entertainer demands a very high appearance fee, a small venue will have to charge so much per seat, or lose so much money, that in practice he will not go there. By contrast, the cost of running a large theatre, which will be at least £10,000 per week, makes it unlikely that its management will take many experimental risks. In this context, the role of subsidy is to widen the extent to which risks are possible, though in practice there is regrettably no correlation between the size of a theatre's subsidy and its willingness to experiment, as most highly subsidised venues demonstrate by their consistent conservatism. West German theatre, for example, the most heavily subsidised in the world, has no commensurate policy of promoting new works by living authors. It is the technicians and administrators who benefit most.

Complementary to the inherent conservatism of large venues is the power of the financial manager over artistic policy. Put crudely, this means that the demands of the building as building tend, in the distribution of resources, to triumph over what goes on in it, administration and technical crews taking up to 60 per cent of budgets.

Behind these issues lies the structure of theatrical management, which has all the hallmarks of the feudal system. A theatrical producer is the baron, who controls money, contracts and policy. He hires staff on a contractual basis that makes them in effect his retainers. They are schooled in obedience to his will and, for all the advances made by actors' trades unions, such as Equity, the aesthetic progress of ensemble acting has not been matched by evolution of financial power. There are still very few actors' co-operatives, and managements of venues show a marked reluctance to deal with them. In Britain, state funding-policy has replicated this form, substituting specialist officers for the barons and in so doing creating an even more feudal structure in the process: for, whereas the baron was ultimately accountable to a public through the box office, the effect of subsidy is to remove even that check from officers. Given the additional bias towards heavy centralisation of funds in London, the effect of subsidy has been to create a top-heavy, unaccountable administration presiding over an impoverished artistic scene.

The combination of managerial policy and overall financial position will determine the size of the performing-company. Only a small number of theatres now are able to sustain a large complement of full-time performers. The smaller the cast the better, which is one reason why two-handers such as *Educating Rita* are received with open arms by managements the world over. Only at the top and the bottom of the performance pyramid, the National Theatre and the school play, do Shakespearian armies look remotely like armies. This is nothing new. In 1620, when the English Comedians staged the battle of the King of England with the King of Scotland, the battle consisted of a set of single combats, the victor in each case running off, changing shields, and re-emerging to fight the next member of the cast. Eventually one person out of the troupe of twelve was left standing: the winner.[12]

BOX-OFFICE APPEAL

The most sensitive and least predictable barometer of success is the box office. True, certain events and acts are guaranteed sell-outs, but only for a given time. The pop market in particular is so volatile that success may vary by the week or even day. Yet even the classic theatre market is highly susceptible to variations in box-office return. The experience is a common one that the same production on tour may do exceptionally well one day and exeptionally badly the next in towns and venues to all intents and purposes identical. Further, in large venues a shift of only 1 per cent in overall attendance may mean a difference of as much as £20,000 in annual turnover, which for most large venues is the difference between success and failure.

Success at the box office may be decisively influenced by three factors: the current level of recognition enjoyed by the author of the play; the current level of television popularity of one of the stars of the show; and the word-of-mouth response to the show as a whole, or to the company's last visit. Audiences tend to reward classics with better attendance than new plays, unless the new plays are by known names or have in their casts some popular actor.

At its worst, likely box-office appeal may so determine a venue's policy that it presents only a bland diet of uncontroversial, neutral material. At its best, however, the box office may be integrated in a wider assessment of community appeal and needs. A loss may be acceptable in the first promotion of a new work or company in the knowledge or belief that a return visit will show far higher returns.

VENUE IMAGE

Mediating between the box-office pressures of baronial theatre management and the interests of aesthetic innovation and marginal or minority-audience tastes may be a consciously determined venue image, influenced by the political climate of its host community and, most notably, by the artistic views of those responsible for it. Ideally, a venue will build up the trust of its audience to the point where its decision to stage a particular production will be guarantee enough of its worth. The problem here is that the typically loyal audience is loyal to an amateur company, and rare are the amateurs that take significant risks. Even the contemporary plays they perform tend to be classics, with West End pedigrees. It is astonishing, given the range of material available, to find countless poor detective plays and endless *Real Inspector Hounds* in the community centres and colleges of the English-speaking world. There is evident safety in a crowd. This is not to argue that a local community has no right to choose what it wishes to see and support. The point is, rather, that laziness and cowardice can be deadlier enemies of performances of quality than poor acting, with the effect that the community is badly served.

Equally deadly is the tendency of professional arts centres to be dominated by small groups of self-congratulatory aficionados, whose parochialism and lack of concern for their audiences renders their work sterile and forbidding to the outsider.

POLITICAL INFLUENCE

There are two principal ways in which politics can affect a venue. First, the local political scene will affect the extent to which subsidy and assistance are available to a venue. Secondly, the ideology of the performers may determine how and what they perform, and whom they invite to share their stage. Artists of all kinds have to intervene in the political process in order to secure resources for themselves, but they have two ways of doing so. They may lobby within a given set of political structures for a place within the list of priorities. Or they may attempt to change the political infrastructure in such a way that a better climate is created for art as a whole. The famous dadaist slogan 'Art is a weapon' underlines

how powerful a political resource the artist has in his own hands –
his art; yet few artists seem willing to be politically engaged.

In one sense, all culture is a product of ideological positions,
whether left, right or centre, so that the refusal of artists to dirty
their hands with politics is an ostrich-like ignoring of political
realities. But, if artists want resources from the state and other
corporate institutions, they have to be prepared to be politically
active on their own behalf. Their general perception of politics as
compromise, the art of the possible, leads them to see a
fundamental incompatibility between artistic excellence and
political mediocrity. Yet this is naïve. Any work of art involves
some form of compromise between imagined ideals and realised
acutalities, whether a compromise of material resources or of time,
or of imaginative energy. In the context of the overall relativity of
any artistic statement, however, this compromise is not necessarily
a defeat: it may simply be a response to simple practicalities. Art
may just as well emerge from the triumph over limitations as from
the chemistry of ideal conditions.

TECHNICAL FACILITIES

Theatres tend to flaunt technical innovations as tribal chiefs wear
bangles: the more you have, the higher your status. The danger is
obvious, and recurrent. The innovations displace the performer
from the aesthetic and the financial centre of attention. Yet it is
usually easier to argue the case for spending money on a piece of
equipment, because the commitment to capital-spending is one-off,
than to do so for budgets relating to performers, who imply
long-term financial obligations. The problem extends to theatre
buildings as a whole. Rich endowments are given to build
monumental theatres, but are not matched by money sufficient to
use them to the full. American university campuses in particular are
prone to this problem.

The role of the performer

What role may the performer and performance play in the cultural
system? At the level of the individual performance, the performer
pleases, and through pleasure instructs, intensifies feeling and
advances the cultural consciousness. In a wider sense, performance
may stimulate, promote and celebrate community.

Pleasing

Pleasing is not fawning. The performer who attempts merely to please betrays his critical, representational distance in trying to be unalloyed pleasure for his audience. Nor is tragedy necessarily 'unpleasant' or 'unpleasing' because it shows horror, pain and suffering. The pleasure we feel may be at the deeper level of recognising the truthfulness of what we are shown, the integrity in moral, political or aesthetic terms of the performed. For it is not the task of the performer to be more or less moral than what he is portraying. If it were, no moral performer could perform Hitler, or Herod. Rather, theatre presents the evidence on which moral, political or aesthetic judgements can be made.

Intensification

The process of intensification may be achieved solely by the acts of designation with which performances begin. But implicit in designation is also defamiliarisation, for the mere act of placing an actant or object on a performance space draws attention to it. Intensification may then be achieved in seemingly opposite ways, by making more familiar, more approachable, or by making strange and unfamiliar. These reactions are complementary. The intense pleasure we may feel in a slight excess of wine may turn to extreme displeasure at over-indulgence. Performers then have the tricky task of intensifying without rendering absurd or deadly. Tragedy in particular is susceptible to falling off into the absurd as one too many bodies to bear is piled up on stage.

Stimulating community

The effectiveness of performance in stimulating a sense of community will be measured directly by the social relationship it generates between audience and performers and the extent to which a sense of community is transmitted through performance. Community-theatre schemes on housing-estates, in which the frequently forbidding atmosphere of recent architectural styles can to some extent be neutralised in the engagement of a community in collective performance, show what can be achieved in this way. At its simplest this may mean the orchestration of a street party, or Bonfire Night. At a more complex level, the community event may involve the performance of a work exploring local tensions and issues, a classic piece of shamanism. Both levels are implied by Rousseau's model of the celebratory stake, analysed earlier, for the stimulation of community comes at the point at which spectators become aware they are performers. This reversal of perspective is the basis of any subsequent audience–performer relations.

Promoting community

Promoting community through theatre has been one of the dominant applications of theatre in this century, from the blueshirts of the Russian Revolution, attempting to use theatre as a direct means of social change, to the play-buses cruising the inner cities. Much of the energy for such theatre comes from the unprovable belief that theatre can make things happen, can effect change. Occasionally there seems evidence to support the case: *Cathy Come Home*, for example, is frequently treated as a piece of television drama that directly effected change. But, considering the sheer number of performances and the volume of material covered, there is statistically every reason to doubt theatre's direct powers of influence. If a climate for change exists, however, a well-staged performance can act as catalyst.

Where notable successes have been achieved is in the use of theatre with the mentally and socially disadvantaged – not simply for therapeutic use, but also in reclaiming an area of expression effectively denied to them by social convention. In effect, theatre becomes a lobbying-instrument, a tool to deal with antipathies and prejudices. The sharper self-image theatre generates among the performers leads to a sharpening of social and political objectives, and to enhanced campaigning for better conditions, rights and status.

Celebrating community

From the classical Athenian festivals, through the guild pageants to the lord mayor's procession and Fourth of July parades, performances have a history of celebrating community. At the civic, tribal and national level, performers are in demand when societal rites of intensification occur. But there is a danger for the performer in seeing these as the ultimate justification of his being, as much recent anthropological research into theatre has tended to argue. In celebrations, the performer is merely an agent in another process, religious or political. The dancer in becoming the dance loses his representational status, and hence his relativising power. All that counts is *the* dance. The community celebrated becomes a community of belief not of art, and, once the belief system has been reaffirmed, the performer is consigned again to decent obscurity.

The courtly clown or jester, and the institution of carnival, were manifestations of particular modes of tension-venting during specific periods of the year. Boys became bishops, the rich served the poor. But far from creating an anti-world, these rites merely reinforced the existing one, the absurdity of the special reversal or roles making all the stronger the existing stereotypes. The 'allowed fool' is privileged. He may slander, rail and curse because ultimately, like Cassandra, he finds no one to listen to his truths. And, as in the storm scene in *King Lear*, when there is real madness in the air the Fool rediscovers his own sanity.

Integration and conflict

The emphasis of this chapter has been on the integrative nature of theatre, but this is at best half of the issue: for theatre emerges out of conflict, both on and off the stage. This conflict is not simply reflected in its content, in action: it also manifests itself in debates about theatrical form, and about dramaturgical strategy. Under the influence of television and the electronic revolution in information technology, theatre is being confronted with challenges and possibilities more profound than at any time since the Renaissance. The audio-visual in our culture is edging the textual to the sidelines, a change from which theatre stands to benefit, if it chooses to do so. But this will entail a reconsideration of its priorities against the background of a prevailing sense in theatre of decline in public esteem and interest. Will it have the energy to reform itself?

Chapter 7

Out of Memory: Towards a New Poetics of Performance (ii)

Conflict is at the centre of the dramatic. Two forces come into opposition and out of opposition emerges action. This opposition may be (1) in the form of a moral dilemma, the confrontation of a good man with an evil destiny leading to moral conflict, suffering and purgation. This is the direction in which Aristotle takes the cathartic view of performance. It may, however, be (2) that the opposition is part of constant dialectic, a continuous cultural dynamic such as Hegel and Marx describe, in which theatrical performance is no different from all other aspects of human life as subject to deep historical laws. Or it may be (3), as Nietzsche describes, a process of seeking complementary oppositions which when in perfect balance fuse into creativity – the complementarity of Apollonian and Dionysian forces, such as reason and passion, form and content, lyric and tragic. These three positions constitute the tradition, the 'memory', out of which the new poetics must emerge, and from which they must also distance themselves.

Catharsis

Aristotle's passing allusion to the purgative effect of tragedy has been at the centre of the theoretical debate about the purpose of performance ever since. The reference is part of the celebrated definition of tragedy:

> Tragedy, then, is an imitation of an action that is serious, complete, and of a certain magnitude; in language embellished with each kind of artistic ornament, the several kinds being found in separate parts of the play; in the form of action, not of narrative; through pity and fear effecting the proper purgation of these emotions.[1]

The definition sets two problems: the first is whether tragedy necessarily imitates anything, rather than being, as Nietzsche proposes, merely itself; and the second, which concerns me here, is the extent to which the purgative effect of tragedy is to be regarded as moral in nature. A little later in *The Poetics*, Aristotle adumbrates the process of catharsis:

> Fear and pity may be aroused by spectacular means; but they may also result from the inner structure of the piece, which is the better way, and indicates a superior poet. For the plot ought to be so constructed that, even without the aid of the eye, he who hears the tale told will thrill with horror and melt with pity at what takes place.[2]

Aristotle distinguishes between the tale and the telling, to the extent that he does not allow that performing *Oedipus* is different from narrating it. There is no doubt that hearing the story of Oedipus is both a horrifying and a pitiable experience: we do not have to see him with bleeding eyes to feel the fear of what he has done. But when we do see him blinded we are confronted with an experience of a different kind from that of moral shock and purgation; his physical disorientation, his weakness and utter reliance on others to lead him, are more eloquent of his fall, more evocative of pity, than any words. Similarly, when Lear starts to tear of his clothes in the storm, his act, though buttressed with words, must be seen to be comprehended. While the mind creates many fears more terrible than the realities which provoke them, there are some realities which are at their most terrible when we see them.

Aristotle is right to argue that the mere representation of tragic images on stage with no foundation in psychological, aesthetic or moral conflict will leave audiences generally unimpressed. Acts of stage violence and horror have greatly diminished impact if dissociated from the conflicts which lead to their occurrence. When we watch Oedipus, it is his psychological and moral conflict which first engages us, his physical suffering second. The storm scene in *King Lear* would be merely grotesque farce if it occurred early in Act I. Aristotle is also right that witnessing such acts is frightening, a challenge to our moral sensibility, a confrontation with the limits of what it is possible for humankind to feel. But the very extremity of the situation, mad kings stumbling about in the darkness of grief, makes it an insecure basis for any generalisation about its purpose, moral or aesthetic. We may feel pity for these victims of malicious destiny, or fear lest the same happen to us, even though not kings ourselves; or we may feel, as Nietzsche suggested, pure incomprehension, a sense of pointlessness.

One evident reason why the cathartic theory has remained so influential is its affinity with the consolatory Christian attitude to suffering, that suffering has some purpose. Through sacrifice and pain we come closer to the pains of Jesus, by whose selflessness we are redeemed. Aristotle may not be arguing that Oedipus redeems his people by his sacrifice: he patently does not. But in the purgation of Oedipus's moral consciousness, in which we as audience become engaged, is a model of how we ourselves might respond to grief and suffering. Christianity reinforces the implication that suffering ennobles, enjoining us not to seek to understand the ways of God, but merely, like Job, to accept them.

Gestus

While agreeing with Aristotle's emphasis on the need for magnitude in an action, theatre's function for Brecht is not to teach morals, the fit behaviour of an individual in conflict with his destiny, but to convey a specific class-based ideology: this ideology is of such significance that it cannot risk being falsified or ironised, which can easily happen in performance. So he developed a theory of performance, called *epic theatre*, predicated on communicating directly and unequivocally the principles of Marxism–Leninism in his plays. This theory is expressed in two practical principles, *gestus* and the *alienation effect*.[3]

The concept of gestus is analogous to that of the indivisibility of 'expression', a combination of action and speech containing a single, unfalsifiable message. The gestus may be a short incident in a play, as when Ui is taught to act like Caesar, but it may also be a whole play, in the way that *The Life of Galileo* teaches us about the relationship between scientific advance and religious, social and political conservatism. In concept, the theory of gestus proceeds from the belief that action, especially movement and gesture, is less easily falsifiable than speech, and therefore a sounder basis on which to build ideological teaching. This imperative for truthfulness is then reinforced by the *alienation effect*, whose purpose is constantly to remind the audience that what is being shown is show, is theatre. Neither performers nor audience are permitted identification with characters; everything exists on a purely representational level. Techniques such as sudden interruptions of one action by another, or by song, or by breaches of established conventions of character, focus the attention on the ideological content rather than their theatrical form.

The effects of Brecht's theory are summarised in Walter Benjamin's seminal essay 'What is Epic Theatre?', to which the reader is referred.[4] On the one hand, it changes the equation of 'world = stage' to 'world = exhibition hall': 'Brecht's theatre no longer represents to its audience the boards that symbolise the world, a place of thraldom, but rather a well-situated exhibition hall.'[5] This is close to the territory Beckett explores in *Breath*, though approached from a different direction. On the other hand, it affects the way both directors and performers conceive of their tasks:

> The director no longer gives the actors directions in how to create theatrical effects but rather intellectual propositions to which they must address themselves. The actor by contrast, is no longer to be an imitator trying to get inside a part, but rather an official who is there to make an inventory of the role.[6]

The theory has a number of other practical effects as well as this detached, alienated performing-style. There are to be no tragic heroes, because individual tragedy distracts from the class objective, and because tragedy creates tension in audiences, which is antipathetic to ideological teaching. Theatre itself is not to be moral in atmosphere, not a place of ritual and high morals, but a place of entertainment, where the audience is relaxed, smoking and drinking, feeling at home. To boost morale and to encourage participation in the wider ideological battle of which performance is a part, plays are to be optimistic in nature.

The theory is weak in three respects. In practice, audiences find it hard to view even Brecht's own plays with the detachment he asks for – mainly because, as I have argued earlier, all performing combines the detachment Brecht advocates with the engagement associated with naturalism. Brecht rewrote *Mother Courage*, for example, to make the eponymous protagonist less sympathetic than the first audiences felt her to be; but, rewrite as he could, nothing could prevent audiences from feeling pity for her in the closing scene, when, all alone, she is left dragging a heavy cart. Our whole culture, in which helping old ladies on their own is amongst the highest social duties, would have to crash about our ears before we could react otherwise.

But even the assumption underlying the gestus theory is open to doubt: the assumption, that is, that movement and action are less falsifiable than words. In *Othello*, Shakespeare shows us how a man of action, Othello, is so influenced by a man of words that actions themselves no longer mean to the observer what they do to the protagonists. In particular, Iago has made such play of Desdemona's feelings towards Cassio that he can get Othello to misread a 'dumb-show' engineered by Iago. Iago and Cassio are talking about Bianca while Othello watches:

> OTHELLO.   Now he importunes him
>   To tell it o'er. Go to; well said, well said.
> IAGO.   She gives it out that you shall marry her.
>   Do you intend it?
> CASSIO.   Ha, ha, ha.
> OTHELLO.   Do you triumph, Roman? Do you
> triumph?   (IV.i.113–18)

In this instance, the falsification takes place in the mind, not on the stage itself, and Shakespeare points out that, however clear an action may be, it is not the action itself that determines the way it is interpreted but the expectations of the beholders. In *Othello*, Shakespeare gives us an object lesson in our own manipulability.

Finally, the optimism embodied in the principles of epic theatre is both hard to detect in Brecht's plays and improbable to audiences scarred by social and political conflict and economic decline. To them Nietzsche's defiant pessimism perhaps seemed closer to the truth.

Aesthetic

The position Nietzsche takes in *The Birth of Tragedy* is that conflict exists on an aesthetic rather than a moral level. Starting with the parable of the encounter of King Darius with Silenus in the forest, Nietzsche constructs his 'anti-world' as an aesthetic answer to the failures of both morality and political ideology to make adequate sense of life. The best thing for a man is not to be born, Silenus tells the King, and the next best thing is to quit life as soon as possible.[7]

Only when we have accepted that life has no meaning can we respond to life through art. Out of the complementary balance of aesthetic forces, as symbolised by the gods Apollo and Dionysus, springs the *Ur*-creative, the spirit of music; and on this heard or intimated music is built an aesthetic 'score'. Just as music can contain no explicit moral, but is moral only in as far as we choose it to be so, so all art exists independent of moral values or purposes.

The attraction of Nietzsche's position is a double one: the self-evident failure of all ideologies, so far at least, to answer the problems of the present world must give us pause when we seek consolation in human moralities and belief systems. But the position also places art and the aesthetic at the very centre of life, which for the artist is a rewarding place to find it. Not least for this latter reason has Nietzsche been so influential on the artists of our century. The difficulty is obvious: how do we accept that life has no meaning and that it is better not to be born when birth is one of the few things we all have in common? It seems inconceivable, looking up at the stars, or watching children at play, that to end life as soon as possible is the only wise move for man. Is all that we do a response to our fear of death?

In a sense, the entertainment case for theatre is closest to Nietzsche's: performance for performance's sake. Do not seek for meanings of a political moral kind: relax, escape, enjoy the show. Where Nietzsche dissents most obviously from this stance is in the passionate seriousness with which he views 'entertainment'. For all entertainment constitutes the integration of the Apollonian urge to

form and the Dionysian release of social and societal tensions, a
liberation into art, of whatever quality, of the submerged desires
and aggressions of our culture. Tragedy lurches on the edge of
farce; farce is tragedy from another perspective: however serious or
frivolous the performance form, each manifests the unmistakable
chemistry of Apollo and Dionysus.

A new Poetics: concentration, intensification, relativisation

In the *Empty Space*, Peter Brook argues persuasively for a new
dramaturgy 'beyond Beckett and Brecht' which integrates the
detachment of Brecht's epic-theatre style with the sincerity of
naturalistic acting.[8] My argument that performance is
simultaneously representation and being takes a similar position,
but it goes further in that such a new dramaturgy will only be
possible on the basis of innovation in theatrical form. If formal
innovation is to succeed, it will have to break not only with the
classical architecture of beginning, middle and end, as advocated by
Aristotle, but also with episodic theatre of the Brechtian kind. It
must permit the possibility of moral and political meaning, but not
depend on, or be circumscribed by any single ideology.

Form and innovation

The formal advance of greatest significance to film is the technique
of *montage*, in which, rather than by means of classical scenic
exposition, logical sequencing of plot and necessity of historical
design, a rapid series of disjunct, impressionistic shots are strung
together in a practical realisation of dynamic iconography. At its
most radical, the result is work such as Man Ray's and Max Ernst's
Ballet mécanique, a filmic collage blending figurative and abstract,
real and imagined. The work is so conceived as to maximise the gaps
and indeterminacies on which the view has to exercise his
imagination, with the result that lazy viewers soon close their eyes.

It was Sergei Eisenstein,[9] originally trained as a theatre director,
who made the decisive breakthrough with montage, partly out of
frustration with the restrictions naturalism had imposed on the
theatre. For Eisenstein, performance space had to resemble the
circus ring, a neutral place in which acts of widely differing kinds
could happen in quick succession. Audiences were not disturbed by

such differences, because the ring itself and the conceptual framework of the circus gave an aesthetic continuity to them. Indeed, the variety and radical shifts in style were the basis of the show's appeal. Not finding this freedom and flexibility in theatre, Eisenstein turned to film, writing a new cinematic syntax in the process.

The current structure of the television day is perhaps closest in concept to Eisenstein's circus ring: different genres of programme, interspersed with adverts, announcements, weather forecasts and news, follow each other with no necessary or logical sequence. What gives them coherence is the fact that they all reach their audience in the same manner and in the same place. Television-viewing is determined by slots: the news slot, the film slot, the drama slot, the sports slot. No one questions the juxtaposition of such slots, even when they can be as crass as the kitchen-bleach adverts that were shown in the middle of a news programme about the massacre of Palestinian refugees in Beirut. The implication is that television audiences perceive slots as discontinuous and do not carry the information content of one slot across into the next.

Theatre audiences, by contrast, perceive theatre to be continuous in the sense that what they see first influences directly what they see next – audiences become educated in ways of responding in the course of a play, as, for example, in the classic use of the running gag as a comic device. Complex plays depend for comprehensibility on the perceptual continuity audiences bring to the varying sequence of scenes. Yet not all theatrical-performance forms are continuous: variety-shows, for example, are split up into slots, and this generic shape makes them natural successes on television, while continuous televised drama frequently fails.

The challenge to the performer is to use the now-established discontinuous aesthetic of television as the basis of experiment in theatre, for in the dialectics of television and theatre, recorded and live performance, structural discontinuity and perceptual continuity, lie the potential for a new performance mode as popular as television and as challenging as traditional live theatre. Signs of innovation are evident in the rock concert, itself a slot-based genre, each number a different slot, where the integration of live music, light show, dance and screened video suggests a form of *Gesamtkunstwerk* true in grandiose spirit to its Wagnerian ancestor, if different in style.

Through form to relativity

The neglected director, contemporary both to Brecht and
Stanislavski, in whose works such a dramaturgy can be seen in
embryo is Max Reinhardt. Reinhardt's aesthetic attitude as director
was to stage each play as it seemed internally to demand, rather
than to overlay it with a specific naturalistic or epic style. The result
was an unparalleled series of performance successes, far greater
than either Brecht's or Stanislavski's.

Reinhardt summarised his position in this way:

> How to make a play live in our time, that is decisive for us. The
> Catholic Church which aims at the most spiritual, the most
> supernatural, does so by means which appeal directly to our
> senses . . . it surrounds us with the mystical dimness of its
> cathedrals; it charms our eye . . . it fills our ear . . . it stupefies us
> by the odour of its incense. And in such an atmosphere of
> sensuousness, the highest and the most holy reveals itself to us.
> We reveal ourselves and we find the way to our innermost being,
> the way to concentration, to exaltation, to spiritualisation.[10]

He begins by identifying the primacy of the senses – first the eye,
then the ear and nose – to the theatrical process. He then locates this
sensory data in a threefold sequence, *concentration*, *exaltation* and
spiritualisation. His terms are inimical to the heterodox nature of
theatrical as opposed to religious truth, and I am doubtful whether
the purpose of one behavioural form, theatre, can be argued to
promote another. But the sequence suggests a secular alternative
on the basis of which a new dramaturgy may be conceived:
concentration, *intensification* and *relativisation*.

Concentration

The designation of space, time and actant with which performance
begins is *de facto* one of concentration. Boundaries around space
time and actant *concentrate* our attention on them, by establishing
their distinctness from the world around them. This term we may
therefore take over unaltered from Reinhardt's scheme.

Intensification

The *exaltation* Reinhardt describes is more religious than theatrical
in nature, a lifting out of the usual, a transcending of worldly limits.

But theatre's purpose is less to transcend than to intensify, to make us more aware of the extraordinariness of what we take for granted. So, instead of exaltation, the new dramaturgy leads to *intensification*. The effect of concentration is to intensify our perception of what we are shown. A mediating-point between theatre and ritual is *rites of intensification*,[11] rituals which are connected with recurrent feast days and festivals in the life of a culture. Christmas, Easter, birthdays, sabbaths – all have intensificatory rituals attached to them to reinforce their personal or social significance; they manifest themselves in unusual 'holiday' behaviour, special clothing, giving gifts, eating special foods and journeying to meet the kinship or peer group. Theatrical performance draws on equivalent rituals, and concerns itself with the tensions the rites of intensification are designed to vent and control. But performance has none of the certainty of outcome of such rites, nor the inherent purpose of affirming the existing state of things.

Performance shares with rites of intensification their enhancement of *communitas*, that sense of communal identity referred to in the discussion of proxemics in Chapter 2. It may achieve this by making the members of an audience feel part of a participatory group. But there are other ways. Groups sharing a common physical or political disadvantage may use theatre as a means to an end, the promotion of their interests in the wider community. Theatre may also help a geo-political community establish a higher level of communal identity and purpose, as when a community-theatre project generates a sense of co-operation in a village or housing-estate. In such applications of theatre to a social purpose, there is more to performance than affirming an existing order; rather, performance enables a transition to occur from one state of *communitas* to a higher one. In this it is more analogous to a *rite of passage*.

Those ceremonies by which parts of, or whole, cultures irreversibly change state are known as *rites of passage*. Weddings, for example, celebrate the passage from childhood into parenthood, as represented physically in the loss of virginity. Wars may conceal more complex and turbulent rites of passage in which cultures in irreconcilable conflict progress, at whatever cost, to a new state. Paradoxically, performances of theatrical works within such rites have the effect not of passage but of intensification, whereas, in societal rites of intensification, theatre may effect a rite of passage.

Relativisation

Reinhardt's third concept, spiritualisation, directs the theatre's attention away from theatre towards religion. But, as I have argued, the two part company over the concept of relativity, and it is *relativisation* that I propose as the third level of the dramaturgical sequence. While the object of religion is to lead the believer up and out of the real world, the object of performance is to take the audience deeper into the real by presenting other facets and versions of it. In this way theatre establishes itself as, and at, the leading edge of cultural consciousness, having the function of cultural agent for the continuous assimilation and accommodation of new skills.

Relativisation: extending the repository of cultural possibility

In the view of Claude Lévi-Strauss, conflict is not merely at the heart of performance: it constitutes the basis of all social activity. He regards the act of belonging to a society as one of simultaneously wishing to destroy it: all of us wish to impose ourselves on our culture, and to do so we have to deconstruct the existing forms and reconstruct them in our own image. The manifestations of this conflict exist on three levels, each of which has its own modes of representation: these are *kinship*, *economics* and *language*. Competing social groups will compete for power and dominance in one or more of these areas. Parents will dispute for power within the kinship structure with their children, and at key times such as marriage, when children turn into parents, emotions and tensions are at their highest. Much Shakespearian comedy locates the problem of marriage within a conflict with the parental generation. Families or clans will compete for economic, and hence political, power by dispossessing one another through intrigue, war or assassination. Machiavelli identified how close the ties between kinship and economics are, and sexual and political struggle are commonly interfused.

These struggles are conducted not merely through language, but also for control over it. Hitler established his domains not just over the German political and military establishment: he also changed the definitions of the German lexicon in such a way that 'Jew' and 'Communist' became explicitly synonymous with 'treachery', 'enemy', that which is to be destroyed. In South Africa, 'black' is defined by the ruling establishment as inferior in a similar manner. Theatre draws heavily on the will to linguistic power, and, as Dario Fo expresses it, linguistic power is the source of political power.

Theatre does not just give expression to these conflicts: by their ritual enactment, they are at the same time vented in the relative safety of performance as opposed to the explicit conflict of war. This power of theatre is equivalent to that of *shamanism* in many cultures, the power of healing through a mixture of applied psychology, ritual and magic. This power depends utterly on the complicity of both the shaman and patient in the healing-process, and like theatre recognises the simultaneity of being and representing in the way the shaman embodies the patient's illness. E. T. Kirby describes this kind of activity as 'primordial clowning':

> Primordial clowning is everywhere associated with the irrational and with the demonic. The shamanistic clown societies of the Southwest are sacred because they are associated with the anti-world, an anarchy identified with death which is opposed to the order established and maintained in ceremonies by the benevolent masked gods. One of the clown's functions is to parody the dances of the masked gods while they are in progress.[12]

Earlier in this book I differentiated between the heterodoxy of theatre and the orthodoxy of religion, which heterodoxy emerges from such parody as Kirby refers to here. In suggesting a shamanistic function for theatre, however, I am not reversing that earlier argument. I do not believe theatre to be merely parodic. Theatre, like shamanism, is capable of releasing tension through parody, and the purpose of parody is to generate what Kirby calls an 'anti-world'. Where theatre makes an important transformational leap away from shamanism is that its creation of not just one 'anti-world' but of a potentially infinite variety of such worlds.

The process by which theatre generates these anti-worlds is twofold. First, within an existing system there can be a *substitutive transformation*. Theatre operates within a given cultural system. By substituting new elements of that system, it generates transformations of a kind that relativise the identity of the initial system. Bottom, a man, is given an ass's head, and when we see him in this transformed state we begin to wonder whether he is a man with an ass's head or an ass with a man's body. His identity becomes a matter of choice, not necessity. Secondly, theatre may generate a new system, a possibility Lévi-Strauss denies:

> The customs of a community, taken as a whole, always have a particular style and are reducible to systems. I am of the opinion that the number of such systems is limited and that – in their games, dreams or wild imaginings – human societies never create absolutely, but merely choose certain combinations from an ideal repository that it should be possible to define . . . .[13]

Lévi-Strauss's analogy is from both language and chemistry, but he forgets that in both areas new elements are constantly being added which enrich the old system and force it into a new constellation. Bottom transformed is such a new element in the world of Athens, a hybrid being integrating the man and the ass, the sort of mutant from whom new species grow. His very existence as man–ass denies the finity of the cultural repository, for he is not merely a combination of existing elements, but an entirely new one.

Notes

Chapter 1. All in War with Time: To Perform or not to Perform

1. Horace, *Odes*, III, xxx, in *The Odes, Carmen Saeculare and Epodes*, ed. E. C. Wickham (London, 1904) I, n.p.
2. William Shakespeare, Sonnet 15, in *The Complete Works*, ed. Peter Alexander (London, 1951) p. 1310. All Shakespeare references are to this edition.
3. Plato, *The Republic*, tr. with an intro. by H. D. P. Lee (Harmondsworth, 1955) pp. 383–6.
4. St Augustine, *Concerning the City of God against the Pagans*, tr. H. Bettenson, with an intro. by David Knowles (Harmondsworth, 1972) pp. 43–4, 56–8, etc.
5. A classic Elizabethan defence of theatre in these terms is Thomas Heywood, *An Apologie for Actors* (London, 1612) *passim*.
6. Aristotle, *The Poetics*, tr. with critical notes and intro. by S. H. Butcher (London, 1936).
7. For a recent study of Jesuit drama see William H. McCabe, *An introduction to Jesuit Theatre*, ed. Louis Joldani St Louis, 1983) *passim*.
8. Aristotle, *The Poetics*, p. 23.
9. The limits of semiotic analysis may be seen, for example, in the notational system offered in Keir Elam, *The Semiotics of Theatre and Drama* (London, 1980) pp. 192–207.
10. Research into the area of neuro-physiology is currently being conducted at the Theaterwissenschaftliches Institut, University of Munich, by Dr Heribert Schälzsky and his colleagues.
11. Aristotle, *The Poetics*, p. 111, on the quality of tragic poetry, and p. 89, on the relationship between poetry and history.
12. Cf. C. L. Barber, *Shakespeare's Festive Comedy* (Princeton, NJ, 1959) pp. 6ff.
13. Cf. Mikhail Bahktin, 'On Carnival and the Carnivalisation of Literature', in *The Work of François Rabelais and the Popular Culture of the Middle Ages and the Renaissance* (Moscow, 1965).
14. Aristotle, *The Poetics*, p. 25.

15. Cf. Pierre Corneille, 'Discours des trois unités, d'action, de jour et de lieu', in *Writings on the Theatre*, ed. H. T. Barnwell (Oxford, 1965) p. 64. See also his 'Examen' to *La Suivante*, in *Theatre complet de Corneille*, ed. Maurice Rat (Paris, n.d.) p. 317.

Chapter 2. This Huge Stage: A New Poetics?

1. Aristotle, *The Poetics*, pp. 29–31.
2. James Boswell, *Life of Johnson*, Everyman edn, 2 vols (London, 1949) I, 225.
3 Cf. Elam, *The Semiotics of Theatre and Drama*, p. 3.
4. Peter Brook, *The Empty Space* (London, 1968) p. 63.
5. John Keats, *The Letters*, ed. Maurice Buxton Forman, 2 vols (London, 1931) I, 77.
6. Jean-Jacques Rousseau, *Lettre à D'Alembert*, with an intro. by Michel Launay (Paris, 1967) p. 234. I am indebted to David Bradby for the translation.
7. The extent of this movement may be measured by the rapid growth of *The Alternative Theatre Handbook*, ed. each year by Catherine Itzin (Eastbourne, 1979–).
8. For a useful summary of proxemics see Elam, *The Semiotics of Theatre and Drama*, pp. 62–9. The originator of the discipline is E. T. Hall, and the reader is directed to his seminal works *The Silent Language* (New York, 1959) and *The Hidden Dimension* (New York, 1966).
9. For Hall's work see previous note.
10. George Bernard Shaw, *Caesar and Cleopatra: A History*, with intro. and notes by A. C. Ward (London, 1960) p. 16.
11. Christopher Marlowe, *Dr Faustus*, ed. Roma Gill (London, 1965) pp. 82–8 [v.ii].
12. Georg Büchner, *Leonce und Lena*, *Sämtliche Werke und Briefe*, Hamburger Ausgabe, ed. Werner Lehmann, (Hamburg, 1967–) I, 120. The translations from Büchner are my own.
13. Bede, *A History of the English Church and People*, tr. Leo Sherley-Price, rev. R. E. Latham (Harmondsworth, 1968) p. 127.
14. Plato, *The Republic*, pp. 278–9.

Chapter 3. I Engraft You New: Learning to Perform

1. The research in progress is being conducted by Paul Ekmann in San Francisco and Heiner Ellgring in Munich.
2. The most useful starting-point for the relationship between drama and developmental psychology is Jean Piaget, *The Moral Judgement of the Child*, tr. Marjorie Gabain (London, 1932) *passim*.
3. Ruth Ault, *Children's Cognitive Development* (New York, 1977) *passim*. This is a very useful introduction to both Piaget's and the American school of developmental psychology.
4. Ibid., pp. 18–22.
5. Aristotle, *The Poetics*, p. 15.

6. *The Works of Francis Bacon*, ed. James Spedding, Robert Leslie Ellis and Douglas D. Heath (London, 1857–74) IV, 496.
7. Cf. Herbert Marcuse, *Eros and Civilisation* (London, 1969) pp. 30–5. The terms originate in Sigmund Freud's work, but my use is intended to echo Marcuse's discussion.
8. Friedrich Schiller, *Über die aesthetische Erziehung des Menschen in einer Reihe von Briefen*, in *Werke in Drei Bänden*, ed. Herbert G. Goepfert (Munich, 1966) II, 445–520. The translations are my own.
9. Ibid., p. 481.
10. Ibid., p. 517.
11. Bertolt Brecht, *Gesammelte Werke in 20 Bänden*, Werke Ausgabe Edition Suhrkamp, ed. Elizabeth Hauptmann (Frankfurt, 1967) IX, 762, 764. All translations from Brecht are my own.
12. Rudolf Laban, *Modern Educational Dance*, 3rd edn, rev. with additions by Lisa Ullmann (London, 1975) *passim*.
13. Brecht, *Gesammelte Werke*, IV, 1769.
14. Laban, *Modern Educational Dance*, pp. 29–51.
15. G. E. Lessing, *Hamburgische Dramaturgie*: 'Vierzehntes Stück, den 16 Junius, 1787', in *Gotthold Ephraim Lessings Sämtliche Schriften*, 23 vols, ed. Franz Muncker, 2nd edn (Stuttgart, 1886) IX, 239. The translation is my own.
16. See, for example, Edward Braun, *The Theatre of Meyerhold: Revolution on the Modern Stage* (London, 1979) pp. 23–4.
17. Karl Gutzkow, letter to Büchner, in Büchner, *Werke*, II, 490–1).
18. Edward Gordon Craig, *On the Art of the Theatre* (London, 1914) pp. 59–94.

Chapter 4. Naught but Shows: Towards a New Poetics of Performance (i)

1. Anton Chekhov, *Uncle Vanya*, in *The Cherry Orchard and Other Plays*, tr. Constance Garnett (London, 1935) p. 136.
2. For Inigo Jones's work on the seventeenth-century masque form see Roy Strong and Stephen Orgel, *Inigo Jones: The Theatre of the Stuart Court*, 2 vols (London, 1973).
3. See below, p. 149.
4. Cf. Adolphe Appia, *Die Musik und die Inscenierung* (Munich, 1899), available now in English as *Music and the Art of the Theatre*, tr. R. W. Corrigan and Mary Dirks (University of Miami Press, 1962); and Craig, *On the Art of the Theatre*.
5. John Milton, *Samson Agonistes*, in *The Poems of John Milton*, ed. John Carey and Alisdair Fowler (London, 1968) p. 349.
6. Büchner, *Werke*, I, 131.

Chapter 5. Their Brave State: Movement and Sound

1. Aristotle, *The Poetics*, p. 69.
2. Cf. Johannes Crüger, 'Englische Komödianten in Strassburg in Elsass', *Archiv für Litteraturgeschichte*, XV (1887) 115, n.2.

3. Harold Pinter, *The Homecoming* (London, 1965) pp. 24–5.
4. Büchner, *Werke*, I, 39.
5. Brecht, *Gesammelte Werke*, IV, 1433.
6. Ben Jonson, *The Complete Plays*, Everyman edn, 2 vols (London, 1964) I, 499.
7. David Storey, *Home* (London, 1970) p. 56.
8. Richard J. Anobile (ed.), *Why a Duck? Visual and Verbal Gems from the Marx Brothers' Movies*, with an intro. by Groucho Marx (London, 1972) p. 41.
9. Lord Byron, *Poetical Works*, ed. F. Page, new edn ed. John Jump (Oxford, 1970) p. 83.
10. T. S. Eliot, *The Complete Poems and Plays* (London, 1969) p. 263.
11. Jonson, *Complete Plays*, I, 404.
12. *The Letters of Gerard Manley Hopkins to Robert Bridges*, ed. with notes by Claude Collier Abbot (Oxford, 1935) pp. 43–7.
13. Eliot, *Poems and Plays*, p. 239.
14. Cf. Ezra Pound, *The ABC of Reading* (London, 1961) p. 31, where Pound quotes Dante on the same subject.
15. John Arden, *Serjeant Musgrave's Dance*, in *Plays: One* (London, 1977) p. 109.
16. Chekhov, *The Cherry Orchard*, p. 78.
17. *Von dem verlornen Sohn* (1620), in Manfred Brauneck (ed.), *Spieltexte der Wanderbühne*, I: *Englische Comedien und Tragedien*, Ausgaben Deutscher Literatur des XV. vix XVIII. Jahrhunderts (Berlin, 1970) p. 99.

Chapter 6. Cheered and Checked: Performers and Audiences

1. William Wycherley, *The Country Wife*, ed. John Dixon Hunt (London, 1973) p. 7.
2. The origins of reception theory lie in the work of Hans-Robert Jauss, *Literaturgeschichte als Provokation* (Frankfurt, 1970) *passim*.
3. Carl von Clausewitz, *Vom Kriege*, 19th Jubilee edn, ed. Werner Hahlweg (Bonn, 1980) pp. 1179–80.
4. Ben Jonson, *Bartholomew Fair*, New Mermaid edn, ed. Maurice Hussey (London, 1964) p. 9.
5. Cervantes, *The Adventures of Don Quixote*, J. M. Cohen (Harmondsworth, 1961).
6. Ibid., pp. 638–45 [pt II, chs 25–6].
7. Henry Fielding, *Tom Jones* (Harmondsworth, 1966) pp. 757–60 [bk XVI, ch. 5].
8. Schiller, *Über naive und sentimentalische Dichtung*, in *Werke*, II, 540–606.
9. Marshall McLuhan, *Understanding Media* (London, 1964) pp. 22–32. McLuhan's summary of the effect of television is on pp. 308–37.
10. The term is McLuhan's and found in *The Medium is the Message* (London, 1964) p. 63.

11. Raymond Williams, *Drama in Performance* (Harmondsworth, 1968) pp. 186–7.
12. Brauneck, *Spieltexte der Wanderbühne*, pp. 262–3.

Chapter 7. Out of Memory: Towards a New Poetics of Performance (ii)

1. Aristotle, *The Poetics*, p. 23.
2. Ibid., p. 49.
3. Brecht's main statements of theory are in *Gesammelte Werke*, XVI, in his dialogue *Der Messingkauf*. The alienation effect (*V-Effekt*) is discussed on pp. 613–31, gestus on pp. 753–4, and white light on pp. 756–7.
4. Walter Benjamin, 'Was ist episches Theater?', in *Versuche über Brecht*, ed. with a commentary by Rolf Tiedemann (Frankfurt, 1966) pp. 7–38. Translations from Benjamin are my own.
5. Ibid., p. 8.
6. Ibid., p. 8.
7. Cf. Friedrich Nietzsche, *The Birth of Tragedy*, tr. with a commentary by Walter Kaufmann (New York, 1967) p. 42.
8. Brook, *The Empty Space*, pp. 85–6.
9. Sergei Eisenstein, *The Film Sense*, tr. and ed. Jay Leyda (London, 1968) and *Film and Form: Essays in Film*, tr. Jay Leyda (London, 1951), give the reader a thorough coverage of the development of the theory of montage out of the theatre, Eisenstein paying particular attention to the audio-visuality of film. His reference to the mobility of the circus appears in a collection of fragments, *Schriften 1/Streik*, ed. Hans-Joachim Schlegel (Munich, 1974) pp. 276–82 [*Theatre as 'Pre-School' of the Image – Sound Counterpoint*, c.1935].
10. Quoted in David Bradby and John McCormack, *People's Theatre* (London, 1979) p. 19.
11. Cf. Arnold van Gennep, *The Rites of Passage* (Chicago, 1908) *passim*.
12. E. T. Kirby, *Ur-Drama: The Origins of Theatre* (New York, 1975) p. 27.
13. Claude Lévi-Strauss, *Tristes tropiques*, tr. John and Doreen Weightman (London, 1973) p. 178.

Select Bibliography

Anobile, Richard (ed.) *Why a Duck? Verbal and Visual Gems from the Marx Brothers*, with an intro. by Groucho Marx (London, 1972).

Appia, Adolphe, *Die Musik und die Inscenierung* (Munich, 1899).

Aristotle, *The Poetics*, tr. with critical notes and intro. by S. H. Butcher (London, 1936).

Artaud, Antonin, *The Theatre and its Double*, tr. Mary Caroline Richards (New York, 1958).

Augustine, St, *Concerning the City of God against the Pagans*, tr. H. Bettenson, with an intro. by David Knowles (Harmondsworth, 1972).

Ault, Ruth, *Children's Cognitive Development* (New York, 1977).

Bakhtin, Mikhail, *The World of François Rabelais and the Popular Culture of the Middle Ages and the Renaissance* (Moscow, 1965).

Barber, C. L., *Shakespeare's Festive Comedy* (Princeton, NJ, 1959).

Benjamin, Walter, *Versuche über Brecht*, ed. Rolf Tiedemann (Frankfurt, 1966).

Berry, Cicely, *Voice and the Actor* (London, 1975).

Braun, Edward, *The Theatre of Meyerhold: Revolution on the Modern Stage* (London, 1979).

Brecht, Bertolt, *Gesammelte Werke in 20 Bänden*, Werke Ausgabe Edition Suhrkamp, ed. Elizabeth Hauptmann (Frankfurt, 1967).

Brook, Peter, *The Empty Space* (London, 1968).

Büchner, Georg, *Sämtliche Werke*, Hamburger Ausgabe, ed. Werner Lehmann, 4 vols (Hamburg, 1967–).

Clausewitz, Carl von, *Vom Kriege*, 19th Jubilee edn, ed. Werner Hahlweg (Bonn, 1980).

Corneille, Pierre, *Writings on the Theatre*, ed. H. T. Barnwell (Oxford, 1965).

Craig, Edward Gordon, *On the Art of the Theatre* (London, 1914).

Diderot, Denis, *Paradoxe sur le comedien* (Paris, 1830).

Eisenstein, Sergei, *Film and Form: Essays in Film*, tr. Jay Leyda (London, 1951).

——, *The Film Sense*, tr. and ed. Jay Leyda (London, 1968).

Elam, Keir, *The Semiotics of Theatre and Drama* (London, 1980).

Eliot, T. S., *The Complete Poems and Plays* (London, 1969).

Goffman, Erving, *Interaction Ritual* (New York, 1967).

Grotowski, Jerzy, *Towards a Poor Theatre*, ed. Eugenio Barba, with a preface by Peter Brook (London, 1969).

Hopkins, Gerard Manley, *The Letters of Gerard Manley Hopkins to Robert Bridges*, ed. with notes by Claude Collier Abbot (Oxford, 1935).

Jauss, Hans-Robert, *Literaturgeschichte als Provokation* (Frankfurt, 1970).

Johnstone, Keith, *Impro: Improvisation and Theatre* (London, 1979).

Jonson, Ben, *Bartholomew Fair*, New Mermaid edn, ed. Maurice Hussey (London, 1964).

———, *The Complete Plays*, Everyman edn, 2 vols (London, 1910).

Joseph, Stephen, *New Theatre Forms* (London, 1968).

Hall, Edward T., *The Silent Language* (New York. 1959).

———, *The Hidden Dimension* (New York, 1966).

Keats, John, *The Letters*, ed. Maurice Buxton Forman, 2 vols (London, 1931).

Kirby, E. T., *Ur-Drama: The Origins of Theatre* (New York, 1975).

Laban, Rudolf, *Modern Educational Dance*, 3rd. edn, rev. with additions by Lisa Ullmann (London, 1975).

Leacroft, Richard, *The Development of the English Playhouse* (London, 1979).

Lévi-Strauss, Claude, *Tristes tropiques*, tr. John and Doreen Weightman (London, 1973).

———, *Structural Anthropology* (New York, 1963).

Marcuse, Herbert, *Eros and Civilisation* (London, 1969).

McCabe, William H., *An Introduction to Jesuit Theatre*, ed. Louis Joldani (St Louis, 1983).

McLuhan, Marshall, *Understanding Media* (London, 1964).

———, *The Medium is the Message* (London, 1967).

Nietzsche, Friedrich, *The Birth of Tragedy*, tr. with a commentary by Walter Kaufmann (New York, 1967).

Pavis, Patrice, *Problemes de semiologie theatrale* (Quebec, 1976).

Piaget, Jean, *The Moral Judgement of the Child*, tr. Marjorie Gabain (London, 1932).

Pisk, Litz, *The Actor and his Body* (London, 1975).

Plato, *The Republic*, tr. with an intro. by H. D. P. Lee (Harmondsworth, 1955).

Pound, Ezra, *The ABC of Reading* (London, 1961).

Reid, Francis, *The Stage Lighting Handbook*, 2nd edn (London, 1983).

Rousseau, Jean-Jacques, *Lettre à D'Alembert*, with an intro. by Michel Launay (Paris, 1967).

Schechner, Richard, *Essays on Performance Theory, 1970—76* (New York, 1977).

Schiller, Friedrich, *Werke in Drei Bänden*, ed. Herbert G. Goepfert (Munich, 1966).

Searle, John, *Speech Acts: An Essay in the Philosophy of Language* (Cambridge, 196).

Shakespeare, William, *The Complete Works*, ed. Peter Alexander (London, 1951).

Stanislavski, Constantin, *An Actor Prepares*, tr. E. R. Hapgood (London, 1937).

——, *Building a Character*, tr. E. R. Hapgood (London, 1950).

Turner, Victor, *The Ritual Process* (Chicago, 1969).

Van Gennep, Arnold, *The Rites of Passage* (Chicago, 1908).

Williams, Raymond, *Drama in Performance* (Harmondsworth, 1968).

Wilshire, Bruce, *Role-Playing and Identity: The Limits of Theatre as Metaphor* (Bloomington, Ind., 1982).

Index